ROME

GUIDE TO THE CITY
DIVIDED INTO 11 ZONES

- *With all the latest updates (page 154)*
- *List of streets (page 165)*

EDIZIONI LOZZI ROMA s.a.s.

Alphabetical index

Rome is situated 41° 53' 54" N. lat., and 12° 59' 53" E. long., on the banks of the River Tiber.

According to Varro's calculations, Rome was founded on April 21ˢᵗ, 753 B.C.

Rome was first governed by Kings (753-510 B.C.); then as a Republic by Consuls (510-30) and finally by Emperors (30 B.C. to 476 A.D.). During the Middle Ages, the Church established its temporal rule and Rome remained the seat of the Papal Court until September 20, 1870 when the Italian army entered Rome and the Eternal City became the capital of a united italy.

The Vatican, a small territory of 0,440 Km² occupied by St. Peter's Basilica, St. Peter's Square and the Vatican Palaces, is under the sovereignty of the Pope, and it has been called the "Vatican City State" since 1929.

ANCIENT ROME - **The Kings of Rome**. According to the legend, the seven Kings of Rome were: Romulus, Numa Pompilius, Tullus Hostilius, Ancus Martius, Tarquinius Priscus, Servius Tullius, and Tarquinius the Proud.

667. Romans and Albans contesting for superiority agreed to choose three champions on each side to decide the question. The three Horatii, Roman knights, overcame the three Curiatii, Alban knights, and unite Alba to Rome.

509. Tarquin the Proud and his family expelled for tyranny and licentiousness; royalty abolished; the Patricians established an aristocratic commonwealth.

The Republic. First period (510-87 B.C.) from the expulsion of Tarquin to the Dictatorship of Sylla. - Second period (87-30 B.C.) from Sylla to Augustus.

496. The Latins and the Tarquins declared war against the Republic and were defeated at Lake Regillus.

477-396. Wars with Veii and the Etruscans. Veii taken by Camillus after ten years' siege.

390. The Gauls, under Brennus, won a remarkable victory over the Romans on the banks of the little River Allia, after which they sacked and plundered Rome. However, they eventually returned to their own land and Rome was gradually rebuilt.

264-146. The Punic Wars, which culminated in the destruction of Carthage, the leading naval power in the Mediterranean.

88-86. Fighting between Marius and Sylla.

82-79. Sylla's dictatorship. Decline of the Republican institutions.

60-53. The First Triumvirate: Caesar, Pompey and Crassus.

58. Caesar's campaigns in Gaul and Britain.

48. Pompey was defeated at Pharsalus.

Caesar was assasinated on March15, 44 (the Ides of March), during a Senate Meeting.

43. The Second Triumvirate: Octavian (the future Augustus), Anthony and Lepidus.

31. Octavian defeated Anthony and Cleopatra at Actium (Greece).

The Empire. The Emperor Octavian (63 B.C. - 14 A.D.) took the name of "Caesar Augustus". The birth of Jesus Christ.

The reign of Augustus coincided with the golden age of Latin literature: this was the era of Writers such as Cicero, Virgil, Lucretius, Horace, Ovid, Livy and Tacitus.

70. Jerusalem was razed to the ground by Titus. Vespasian began to build the Colosseum in 72.

98-117. Under Trajan, the Roman Empire reached its maximum expansion.

117-138. during Hadrian's reign, Rome was at the peak of its architectural splendour.

The Empire began to decline between the 2ⁿᵈ and 3ʳᵈ centuries.

284. Diocletian and Maximian: the first division of the Empire.

313. Constantine the Great allowed the Christians freedom of religious practice. In 331 he transferred the capital of the Empire to Byzantium (Constantitople).

395. The Roman Empire was definitively divided between the East (Arcadius) and the West (Honorius).

404. Transfer of the Capital to Ravenna.

410. Rome sacked by the Goths.

475. Romulus Augustulus, the last Emperor.

476. Odoacer's conqueror of Rome put an end to the Roman Empire in the West.

THE MIDDLE AGES. 493. The Goths established their reign in Italy, defeating Odoacer.

535-553. The Byzantine-Gothic war.

568. The Lombards invaded Italy. It was divided among the Barbarians and the Eastern Empire (the Byzantines).

729. With the donation of Sutri by the Lombard king Liutprandus, the temporal rule of the popes began.

800. On Christmas day, Leo III crowned Charlemagne Emperor of the Holy Roman Empire.

1073-1085. Pope Gregory VII, a fervent and energetic reformer, began his fight against the Emperor Henry IV.

1084. Rome was invaded and sacked by the Romans, led by Robert the Guiscard.

1305. Clement V moved the papal seat from Rome to Avignon, where it remained until 1377.

RENAISSANCE. 1471. The foundation of the Capitoline Museum, the oldest public collection in the world.

1503-1513. Julius II began to pull down the old St. Peter's in order to build the present Basilica, under Bramante's supervision.

1513-1521. Leo X, the son of Lorenzo the Magnificent, made Rome the greatest cultural centre. - Under the pontificate of Leo X the Lutheran Reform began. - The imperial invasion of Italy and the disastrous Sack of Rome (16 May, 1527) put an end to the golden age of the papal city in a nightmare of fire and blood.

THE MODERN AND CONTEMPORARY AGE. 1799. The Jacobine Republic in Rome, pope Pius VI was deported to France.

1800. The First Restoration: Pius VII was re-established in Rome.

1861. On March 27, the Italian Parliament declared Rome the natural and indispensable capital of the new State.

1870. On September 20, Italian troops entered Rome through the breach in Porta Pia.

1929. On February 11, the "Roman Question" between the Church and the State was finally resolved by the Lateran Treaty, which came to be part of the Constitution of the Italian Republic.

1946. In Italy, the Republic was proclaimed in accordance with the June 2 referendum.

1962-65. The Ecumenical Council, Vatican II, was summoned by John XXIII and concluded by Paul VI.

1978. After the death of Paul VI and the pontificate of John Paul I which lasted one month, John Paul II the Polish Pope, acceded to the pontifical throne.

2000. Great celebration of the Holy Year.

2005. The death of John Paul II brought over three million faithful to Rome. On April 19th, the German Joseph Ratzinger was elected Pope with the name Benedict XVI.

1 - Around the Capitol

*Two pictures of the huge
statues of Roman age
representing the Dioscuri
(Castor and Pollux),
defenders of the
Republican Rome.*

♦ **The Capitol**, once sacred to the Romans
and the destination of the triumphal processions
of victorious generals, is today the headquarters
of the Mayor and the Municipality of Rome.

In spite of changing events and historic conditions, the **CAPITOLINE HILL** has remained the basic nucleus of Roman life for thousands of years. It is reached by the grand flight
of steps known as the "Cordonata", built to a
design by Michelangelo especially for the triumphal entry of the Emperor Charles V in 1536.

The bronze statue of **Cola di Rienzo** is by
Masini. It's placed to the left of the *Cordonata*
on fragments of ancient remains, to show that
the last Roman Tribune wanted to re-establish
the Republic on the ruins of the Empire.

Statue of roman age rappresenting the Tiber divinity.

Aerial view of the Capitol.

Above, view of Piazza del Campidoglio, with the Palazzo Senatorio in the background.
Center, the Esquiline Venus *and, below, the* bust of the Emperor Caracalla, *Capitoline Museums.*

At the top of the stairs are the colossal groups of the **Dioscuri**, Castor and Pollux, found near the Ghetto and placed here in 1583 by Gregory XIII. Sixtus V added the **Trophies of Marius** and the **statues of Constantine** and his son Constantine Caesar.

We now reach **Piazza del Campidoglio**, designed by Michelangelo for the munificent Pope Paul III (1534-1549). The old artist placed on a new pedestal the equestrian statue of **Marcus Aurelius** (161-180), the only one of the many bronze equestrian statues once adorning Rome that has survived.

Because the statue was thought for centuries to have represented the first Christian Emperor, Constantine, it escaped the fate of many other statues of pagan emperors, which were destroyed in the Middle Ages.

The completely gilded statue stood at the Lateran in the House of Vero, ancestor of Marcus Aurelius, until Michelangelo had it removed in 1538. In 1997 a copy took the place of the original after a lenghty and delicate restoration.

A large **glass room** was inaugurated in 2005, built from the covering of *Giardino Romano*, destined to be the definitive placement of the bronze equestiral statue of Marcus Aurelius. Architect Carlo Aymonino reproposes the oval space designed by Michelangelo for the capitoline square in the volume of the room, it also embraces the new restoration of the tufa stone foundations of the Capitoline Temple of Jupiter, highlighting them adequately.

This splendid square was conceived by Michelangelo, who also designed the two palaces on the opposite sides of the square, whose divergence creates a widening perspective which is most effective.

Capitoline Museums

In the courtyard of **Palazzo Nuovo** sits the famous statue of **Marforio**, one of the so-called "talking statues" of Rome, like the more famous Pasquino.

A broad stairway leads to the first floor. In the center of Room I lays the **Dying Gaul** a marble copy of the bronze statue from the monument at Pergamon. The simple and natural position of the body, the facial features which express deep anguish while revealing human strength blend marvelously to make this statue one of the most significant expressions of Hellenistic culture.

The well-known group of *Amore e Psyche*, an enchanting Hellenistic creation, shows the chaste kiss of young lovers. The *Satyr Resting* is the best copy of an original in bronze by Praxiteles, the Greek artist who had the divine gifts of tender beauty and grace. Room II, or the "room of the Faun", includes, among other works, the *Laughing Satyr*. Room IV, or the "room of the Philosophers" contains many busts of ancient writers and Greek and Roman warriors. The seated figure at the center of the room is believed to be *M. Claudius Marcellus*, one of the Roman generals of the Second Punic War. Among the many busts, four are of the great epic poet of Greece, *Homer*, traditionally represented as old, poor and blind. *Socrates*, the celebrated Athenian philosopher, is portrayed here with a flattened nose, thick lips and protruding eyes, like a satyr.

Room V, or the "room of the Emperors", contains about eighty busts of Roman emperors, with a few Empresses; it is the most interesting portrait gallery in existence. The "Room of Venus" contains the *Capitoline Venus*, which was found in the Suburra neighborhood in the 17th century.

In the "Room of the Colombe" is the *mosaic of the Doves*, a work so fine that it might easily be taken for a painting. Found at Hadrian's Villa (Tivoli), it was immediately recognized as that which had been described by the naturalist Pliny. The lovely figure of a *Young Girl with a Dove*, clasping it to her breast as a serpent attacks, symbolizes the human soul choosing between good and evil.

Opposite the Capitoline Museum is the **Palazzo dei Conservatori**, which can be reached through the connecting underground passageway that has hosted the **Galleria Lapidaria** since 2005. The Palazzo dei Conservatori, with the *Appartamento dei Conservatori*, official seat of Rome's city government, and the Sala degli Orazi e Curazi which was painted by Cavalier d'Arpino; the baroque painter Cesari worked here on and off for forty years. The other rooms were painted by Laureti, Daniele da Volterra, Caracci and others.

In the "Sala dei Trionfi" is the beautiful bronze statue of the *Cavaspina* (Boy pulling a Thorn from His Foot). The statue portrays a natural, effortless attitude, and is the synthesis of a 5th century B.C. head and a typically Hellenistic body from the 2nd century B.C.

The **Capitoline Picture Gallery** contains, among several important masterpieces of the 16th and 17th centuries: *Romulus and Remus* by Rubens; *Anthony and Cleopatra* by Guercino; The *Kidnapping of Helen* by PaoloVeronese; St. Sebastian by Guido Reni; *St. Petronilla* by Guercino; the *Magdalene* by Tintoretto; the *Gypsy Fortune-teller* and *St. John the Baptist* by Caravaggio; and *portraits* by Van Dyck.

The Dying Gaul, *Capitoline Museums.*

Above, fragments of the colossal statue of Constantine, *Palazzo dei Conservatori.*
In the centre Love and Psyche, *Capitoline Museums.*
Below, model of the Capitol in the Imperial era.

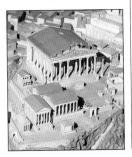

♦ The **Palazzo Senatorio** at the back of the square, was built in the 13th century on the ancient ruins of the Tabularium. Its present façade was designed by Giacomo della Porta and made by Girolamo Rainaldi. Michelangelo designed the flight of steps. The fountain, adorned with three statues, the **Tiber** and the **Nile** on either side and **Rome Triumphant** (of over modest proportions) in the centre, was added in 1588 by Matteo di Castello.

The Senator's Palace is the Mayor's residence. Rising from it is the **Capitoline Tower**, built in 1579 by Martino Longhi, where the famous bell, the "Patarina", once hung.

♦ The two palazzos facing the Piazza del Campidoglio (the Palazzo Nuovo and the Palazzo dei Conservatori) are home to the prestigious MUSEI CAPITOLINI (see box, page 11), the world's oldest public collection whose origins date back to 1471, when Pope Sixtus IV presented the City of Rome with an initial group of bronze statues.

The complex was substantially expanded in 2000, after major restoration work, with the opening to the public of the Tabularium, (connected via a tunnel), the reopening of Palazzo Caffarelli, and the acquisition of Palazzo Clementino.

♦ SANTA MARIA IN ARACOELI rises from the highest point of the Capitoline Hill, where

Visit inside the Basilica of Santa Maria in Aracoeli

There is a side entrance to the church from Piazza del Campidoglio. Inside, just above the door, is a beautiful 13th century mosaic of a *Madonna and Child* and two angels. The nave of the church is supported by 22 columns made of various materials, taken from several pagan temples.

The marvelous 16th century gold coffered **ceiling** was constructed to celebrate the victory of Marcantonio Colonna, who in 1571 led the Christian fleet to victory over the Turks in the famous battle of Lepanto. The interesting, Byzantine-style painting of the *Madonna in Aracoeli*, on the high altar, has been attributed to St. Luke, although scholars date the piece to between the 6th and 11th century. The richly decorated **ambones**, at the end of the central nave, are by Lorenzo Cosmati and his son Jacopo, whose signature is on the right pulpit (12th century).

In the left transept, the octagonal chapel dedicated to *St. Helen* marks the place where the altar raised by Augustus once stood. Just under the altar to St. Helen, at a level 15 cm. (6 in.) beneath the floor, is a white marble altar decorated with sculptures and Cosmatesque mosaics (12th century), that illustrate the Augustan legend as described in the inscription on the table of the altar to St. Helen. The tall, slender statue representing the saint is a contemporary work by Andrea Martini (1972).

there was once the Arx, or citadel of Rome. A legend tells how Augustus raised an altar here to the "Son of God", inspired by an oracle of the Sybil who had foretold of the birth of Jesus. This church thus inherited the glory of the ancient Capitol Hill, becoming the national church of the nobility and people of Rome and the principal seat of the Senate in the middle ages.

The façade of the Basilica of Santa Maria in Aracoeli, facing the Campidoglio, right, and the Vittoriano, left.

The inside of the Basilica of Santa Maria in Aracoeli.

*In April of 2007, on the celebration of the 2760th anniversary of Rome's founding, the statue of the **capitoline Wolf** was moved to a new location in front of the equestrian statue of Emperor Marcus Aurelius in a display case designed by architect Aymonino at the Capitoline Museums. A symbol of the Eternal City, the Wolf is surrounded by illustrated panels and castings that help to retrace the forging technique used: the single pouring of bronze would lead to believe that the statue is from the High Medieval period and not the Republican period (5th century B.C.) as was commonly believed. The stature expresses pride and vitality and seems as if it wants to protect Romulus and Remus, the two twins that it is nursing (15th century).*

The "Capitoline Basilica" is noted for its old reliquaries, tombs, frescoes, gilded ceiling, and ancient relics. Originally it belonged to the Greek monks, but passed to the Benedictines in 883 and finally to the Franciscans in 1250. The main entrance to the church is reached by a **stairway** of 124 steps, built in 1348 as an offering to the Virgin Mary who had liberated the city from a terrible plague and inaugurated by Cola di Rienzo. From the top there is a splendid view of the city. The Romanesque brick **facade**, with traces of mosaics from the late 13th century, was never finished.

♦ PIAZZA VENEZIA takes its name from **Palazzo Venezia**, built in 1455 by the Venetian Pope Paul II (1461-1471), while he was still a cardinal. It was the first great Renaissance palace in Rome, and was richly decorated with outstanding works of art. The structure typifies the early Renaissance period, as it marked the transition to a modern palace from the medieval fortified dwelling, of which it retains certain features.

♦ The **Vittorio Emanuele II Monument** (also called the "Vittoriano"), was designed by Giuseppe Sacconi (1885-1911). It rises from the foot of the Capitol Hill, where it was squeezed into the heart of the city, forever changing

the relationship between this hill and its surroundings. The Venetian sculptor Chiaradia worked for twenty years on the equestrian statue of the king, which was completed by Gallori (1901) after the death of the artist. The elaborate bas-reliefs on the base, which represent the most famous Italian cities, were designed by Maccagnani, who for many years collaborated with Sacconi in carving the three-dimensional ornamentation. The building's two colossal **chariots** are surmounted by winged Victories, whose dark bronze contrasts with the white marble and makes them visible against the Roman skyline. They were made by Carlo Fontana and Paolo Bartolini in 1908. In the center is the **Altar of the Fatherland**, crowned by the statue of Rome, at whose feet since 1921 lies the **Tomb of the Unknown Soldier**.

Two views of the Vittorio Emanuele II Monument, designed by Sacconi, to commemorate Italian unification.

2 - The Colosseum and the Forums

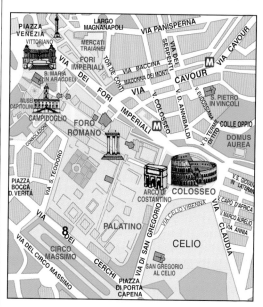

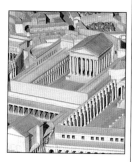

Model of the Forum of Augustus in Imperial era.

Night view of Trajan's Markets.

From Piazza Venezia begins the *Via dei Fori Imperiali*, a broad, straight stretch built in 1932, cutting throught the ruins of the forums from which it takes its name.

♦ TRAJAN'S FORUM. The Emperor M. Ulpius Trajan was born in Italica (Spain) in 53 A.D. The formidable task of his reign was the expansion of the Empire towards the east, beyond Dacia.

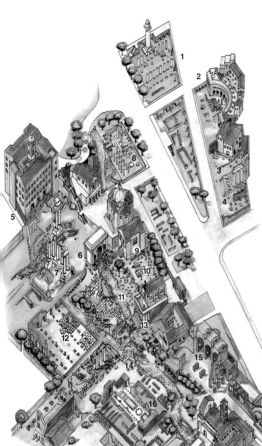

1) Trajan's Forum
2) Trajan's Markets
3) Temple of Mars Ultores
4) Forum of Nerva
5) Tabularium
6) Arch of Septimius Severus
7) Temple of Saturn
8) Forum of Julius Caesar
9) The Curia
10) Basilica Aemilia
11) Via Sacra
12) Basilica Julia
13) Temple of Antoninus
    and Faustina
14) Temple of Vesta
15) Basilica of Maxentius
16) House of the Vestal Virgins
17) Arch of Titus
18) Temple of Venus and Roma
19) Arch of Constantine
20) Colosseum

THE ROMAN FORUM AND THE IMPERIAL FORA

Trajan decided to commemorate his victory by building a Forum that would surpass all other forums in splendor and scale. He entrusted the project to the great architect, Apollodorus of Damascus. By cutting away a good portion of the base of the Quirinal hill, an area twice the size of the existing fora was created; 61 million cubic meters of earth and rock was moved to make way for the Trajan's Forum, which became the most admired place in the city. But the great monument to the victory over the Dacians is the noble **Column**, which after 19 centuries was returned to

Emperor Octavian Augustus (27 BC - 14 AD), Vatican Museums.

Crossing the Forums in Rome. For the 2762nd anniversary of Rome's founding (April 21, 2009), a pedestrian underpass equipped with two elevators will connect the Imperial Forum to the Roman Forum. This at least partially rejoins the two archaeological areas that were divided in the 1930s to build Via dei Fori Imperiali.

its original majesty and antique splendor by careful restoration. The ashes of the emperor were once set into the base of the column and his statue once stood on top. The column consists of 19 blocks of marble and a spiral staircase which leads to the top. The most important part of this historic monument is the helicoidal band of figures that spiral around it, which document the arms, art and costumes of the Romans and Dacians. Included is the bridge that Trajan constructed, the fortresses he attacked, the camps he destroyed and the enemy he put to flight. Previous interpretations of the inscriptions (now confirmed) suggest that the top of the column marked the height of ground level when construction began on Trajan's Forum.

Very little remains of the great buildings which surrounded the Column: the **Basilica Ulpia**, used as a Hall of Justice, the Greek and Latin **libraries**, and the **temple** dedicated to Trajan himself.

♦ Set into the Quirinal Hill is the complex known as TRAJAN'S MARKETS, which consists of a well-preserved, semi-circular, three story structure, and above, a large vaulted hall, which resembles a basilica. The entrance to the complex is in Via IV Novembre.

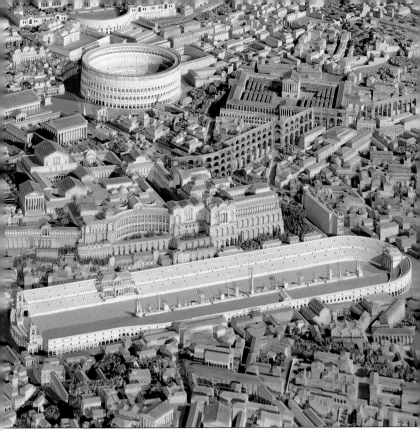

• The FORUM OF JULIUS CAESAR, consecrated in 46 B.C. and later finished by Augustus was the first of the so-called Imperial Forums built with the spoils of victory from the Gallic Wars. Formed by a rectangular piazza surrounded on all sides by porticoes, it had at its center the **Temple of Venus Genetrix**. The Julian family, to which Julius belonged, claimed to originate from Julo, or Ascanius, son of the Trojan hero Aeneas, who according to Homeric mythology was the son of the mortal Anchises and the Goddess Venus. The temple featured many works of art, among them the sculpture of Venus Genetrix by Arcesilao. In its simplicity the Forum of Julius Caesar surpasses the narrow dimensions of the Republican age, and from an historical point of view, underlines the passage to the imperial age by anticipating the monumental complexes built by Caesar's successors. The Forum was expanded by Trajan, who added the Basilica Argentaria.

• THE FORUM OF AUGUSTUS. After the assassination of Caesar, the conspirators Brutus and Cassius went to take possession of the provinces of Syria and Macedonia. In 42 B.C., they

Model of the Roman Forum between the Campidoglio and the Colosseo.

On the previous page, Bust of the Emperor Trajan (98-117 d.C.), Capitoline Museums.

Bronze coin with the profile of the Emperor Vespasian (70 AD).

Roman coin.

led their armies at Philippi against the heirs of Caesar, Octavian and Marc Antony. Just as Julius Caesar took a vow at Farsalo, so Augustus took one at Philippi: in the event of victory, he was to build a temple in a new Forum and dedicate it to Mars, father of the Roman people and God of war. After the victory and the death of the two conspirators, Augustus maintained his vow and built the **Temple of Mars Ultor** (the Avenger) in the center of the new Forum, and inaugurated it on the first of August in the year 2 B.C.

The Forum of Julius Caesar

Gold coin with the profile of the Emperor Tiberius.

Excavations have brought to light magnificent remains of this forum and the gigantic temple, among them three Corinthian columns that once stood 15 meters in height. Augustus was the first Emperor (27 B.C. - 14 A.D.); under his reign, Jesus Christ was born.

♦ THE FORUM OF NERVA. Begun under the Emperor Domitian, this Forum was inaugurated in 97 A.D. by his successor Nerva. Built after the Forums of Caesar and Augustus, it was necessary to make the best of rather limited space, and so it extended in length rather than width.

This was the site of the **Temple of Minerva**,

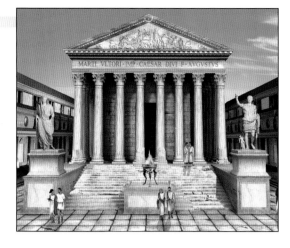

The Temple of Mars Ultor in the Forum of Augustus as it was in Imperial era (above) and as it looks today (down).

which was still standing in 1606 when Pope Paul V had it demolished in order to use its marble to build the Pauline Fountain on the Janiculum Hill. New excavations of the Forum of Nerva seek to reconstruct the historical events and architectural history of the area over the centuries.

◆ THE TEMPLE OF PEACE. The complex of Imperial Forums ended (on the side nearest to the Colosseum) in this temple of enormous proportions.

Excavations in the years 1999/2000 brought to light new finds from these last two complexes, providing a great deal of new information.

◆ At the end of the Via dei Fori Imperiali, between the Esquiline, Palatine and Celian Hills, rises one of the greatest wonders of Roman civilization: the **COLOSSEUM**.

This immense amphitheater, whose imposing remains still allow us to admire its ancient splendor, was begun by Vespasian in 72 A.D. and completed by his son Titus in 80 A.D. It was built by Jewish prisoners.

On the left, portrait of the Emperor Augustus.

It's true name is the "Flavian Amphitheater", though it was commonly called the Colosseum, both for its proportions and its vicinity to the Colossus of Nero. There is hardly a page of Roman history that is not in some way connected to the Colosseum, which became the symbol of the city and its life.

The inside of the Colosseum as it was in Imperial era (above) and as it looks today (down).

A hoist system used for wild animals at the Colosseum.

The Colosseum had the same function as a modern giant stadium, but the favorite spectacles in Roman times were the games of the Circus (ludi circenses), which probably had been invented in the late Republican era, with the intention of cultivating the war-like spirit that had made Romans the conquerors of the world. This was the origin of the professional gladiators, who were trained to fight to the death, while wild beasts of every sort increased the horror of the show. Dion Cassius said that 9000 wild animals were killed in the one hundred days of celebrations which inaugurated the amphitheater. After the animals were killed and removed, the arena was often filled with water in order to stage naval battles. The Emperor Constantine and his successors tried to put an end to the gladiatorial fights, but at first the Romans did not want to give up their customary

shows. At the beginning of the 5th century, a monk called Telemachus came from the east and one day entered the arena and tried to put himself between the gladiators. He appealed to the people to give up their horrid games. The crowd hurled insults, sarcasm, and ultimately rocks, stoning the intruder to martyrdom. But that day the games were brought to an end. The Colosseum is elliptical in shape, 187 meters at its longest end and 155 meters at its shortest. The height of the external ring reaches 50 meters from ground level. It was designed to accommodate an estimated 80,000 spectators. Around the exterior run three orders of arches, respectively adorned with Doric, Ionian and Corinthian columns, and a fourth floor with Corinthian pilasters. Of the 80 arches that make up the elliptical ring, four correspond to the entrances at the four axes, of which only the entrance of honor reserved for the Emperor remains.

The Colosseum as it was in Imperial era (above) and as it looks today (down).

A Roman mosaic with figting gladiators.

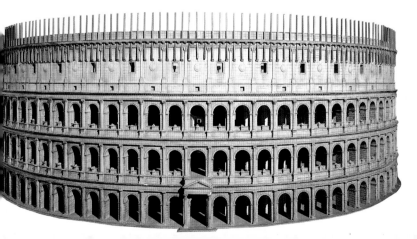

Reconstruction of a section of the Colosseum.

Aerial view of the Colosseum.

The Arch of Constantine, detail.

In the center of the podium, called the *suggestum*, was the Emperor's seat; the rest of the podium was occupied by senators and members of the court. Then came the sections for the knights and civil and military tribunes. The Colosseum was usually uncovered, but in case of rain it was covered by an immense velarium, which was maneuvered by two squads of sailors belonging to the fleets of Ravenna and Cape Misenum. These two squads also took part in the naval battles which were often staged in the amphitheater.

When this amphitheater was in its full glory, it must have been a stupendous site of Roman greatness. But even today, after so many centuries, the Colosseum is the pride of Rome and a marvel to its visitors.

Nonetheless the history of the amphitheater is not without long periods of abandon and neglect. The end of the Roman Empire was marked by two earthquakes (in 442 and 508), which caused great damage to the structure. The Colosseum was nonetheless still in use under Theodoric, ruler of the Romano-Barbaric kingdom of the Goths, who in 523 authorized the staging of the *venationes*, the traditional hunt of the wild beasts. From that point began the total abandon that saw the Colosseum used as a cemetery, a fortress, and above all, after the earthquake of

1349, as a quarry for building materials. The marble which once covered it almost entirely was reused in the busy period of construction during the Renaissance. In order to halt the serious decay of the Colosseum, Pope Benedict XIV (1740-1758) consecrated the old amphitheater by set-

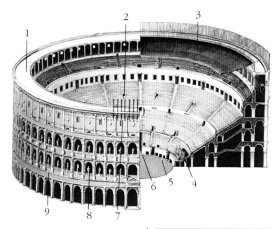

ting up a **Way of the Cross** and raising a cross on the site, which has been connected to thousands of Christian martyrs. Though Christians were certainly among the many who were killed here, there is no historical evidence that Christians were ever massacred in the Colosseum.

• The **Arch of Constantine** was built by the Senate and the Roman people at the edge of the Forum, on the Via Sacra, in memory of the victory over Maxentius at Ponte Milvio in 312. Because it was built largely from pieces from the arches of Trajan and Marcus Aurelius, and from other monuments, this arch was derisively called a "cornacchia di Esopo" (Aesop's Magpie).

• Near the Arch of Constantine are the remains of a circular fountain, called the **Meta Sudans**, which existed from the time of Nero and was later

Cutaway view of the reconstructed Colosseum

1) From the top of the amphitheater, 80 sailors from the Imperial fleet worked the enormous velarium that covered the cavea during the games.
2) Numbered entrances allowed the tens of thousands of spectators to flow easily in and out of the Colosseum.
3) The velarium. Its extension and tensioning lasted four days.
4) Imperial Tribune.
5) Entances for the animals.
6) Entance for the gladiators.
7) 240 supporting shafts were necessary to support the velarium and its cords.
8) Statues of gods. Each arch housed a different statue.
9) The façade, with three orders of arches, were covered in Travertine extracted from caves at Tivoli.

The Arch of Constantine.

The Colosseum in numbers

The Colosseum, or Flavian Amphitheater, was built in just **5 years** of uninterrupted work between 75 A.D. and 80 A.D.

The external ellipse of the arena measures **188 by 156 meters**, and the complex occupies **3357 square meters**.

The façade of the Colosseum is **49 meters** tall, and divided into **three floors** with **80 arches** each, and surmounted by a windowed pilaster attic. **240 corbels** correspond to holes in the attic which housed the shafts that supported the immense velarium (awning). With a surface area of **22,000 square meters**, the velarium covered the arena at a height of about **50 meters**. It was held by cords attached to a metal circle at the center, which had a **circumference of 90 meters**.

The **80 entrance arches** on the ground level were numbered, with the exception of the **four principal entrances** with propylaeums, which were reserved for the emperor, the imperial family and the vestals.

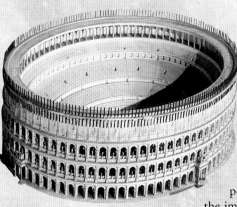

Spectators were given passes which indicated an assigned seat in a particular section, and even the route to that seat. Although entrance was free, seating depended on rigid social divisions.

The **17 rows** of the podium were reserved for the imperial section, magistrates and senators. The low cavea was for the knights; the middle cavea, composed of **19 rows** and **32 entrances**, belonged to the middle class; the "Maenianum summum", or high cavea, formed by **37 rows**, was left to the general public. In total, there were **50 rows in stone**, while the sections for the plebes were built of wood. It is estimated that there was about **30,000 meters** of linear seating space - which would have accommodated **73,000 spectators**.

A great variety of **materials** were used to build the Colosseum: **travertine**, the calcareous stone from the area around Tivoli, to line the façade and for the concentric rings which supported the cavea; **tufa**, or soft volcanic rock, for the foundation and the radial walls; **concrete** to line the vaults of the galleries and arches; **marble** for the splendid finish, the capitals, the statues and the seats of the sections in the first rows; finally, an infinite number of **bricks** for non-structural walls and the screens.

rebuilt by Domitian. It was used by gladiators to wash themselves.

♦ Toward the Via dei Fori Imperiali is a square foundation of travertine, which marks the spot where the **Colossus of Nero** stood. The famous statue was first erected by Nero in the atrium of his Golden House, and later brought here by the Emperor Hadrian to make room for the exceptional twin **Temple of Venus and Roma** which he had designed himself it was the largest, finest religious building in Rome. The columns have been reconstructed and placed to form the portico that once surrounded the temple. In the 7ᵗʰ century the church of Santa Maria Nova was founded on the ruins of the temple of Roma, and rededicated at the beginning of the 18ᵗʰ century to **Santa Francesca Romana**. Relics and objects of interest found in excavations of the Forum area are on display in the "Antiquarium Forense," in the nearby convent annex.

♦ Close by the Coliseum, in the *Colle Oppio* is the access to the celebrated **Domus Aurea** of Nero, an imposing, fantastic group of buildings that extended from the Palatine to the Esquiline, submerged in the greenery of a countryside recreated within the city occupying an extensive area. However, of so many marvels, almost everything disappeared

Ground level passageways of the Colosseum.

Reconstruction of the Temple of Venus and Rome.

Below, an overall view of the immense Piazza del Colosseo. Between Constantine's Arch and the Flavian Amphitheater, the remains of the Meta Sudans and the base of the Colossus of Nero can be seen. In the background, the substantial vestiges of the Temple of Venus and Rome dominate the scene from a broad podium.

*The restoration work done on the **Domus Aurea** documented the abundant use of gold leaf and precious stones to decorate the interiors of Nero's immense palace. Seneca, Nero's counselor and man of letters, described it as "a house resplendent in shimmering gold".*

Marble bust of the Emperor Nero (54-68 AD).

Domus Aurea. The octagonal Hall.

instantly after the death of Nero. His successors wanted to eradicate the slightest memory of these achievements, whose luxury had aroused passionate hatred in Roman hearts. This was the site of the central pavilion, ruined in 104 by a terrible fire. Over it were built the foundations for the construction of the **Bath of Trajan**, of which only a few ruins remain.

The grottoes underneath, once believed to belong to the **Bath of Titus**, were explored by artists of the renaissance who learned here a special decorative style purposely called "grotesque". Here the famous Laocoon was found, and also the enormous porphyry vase (see Vatican Museum) in which Poppea is supposed to have bathed in the milk of one hundred she-asses.

Even in the cold, concise terms of the historian Suetonius, **Nero's Golden House** (Domus Aurea) appears to us like an enchantment from the *Arabian Nights*. It consisted of countless pavillons scattered over an immense park, and was adorned with works of art taken from cities and temples in Greece, while gold and precious stones embellished the walls.

We cannot, of course, describe them fully; we shall only mention the "**crypto-portico**" which isolated the north part of the construction from the hill behind; the names of the Renaissance artist who first went there are carved on the ceiling. It is also worth noticing the great rectangular nymphaeum, culminating in an imposing apse, whose rich decorations have been restored and are clearly visible today. The **room with the golden vault** decorated with the most delicate plaster work; the **octagonal room**, covered by a vaulted pavilion with a central opening. According to the historian Suetonius, the vault slowly rotated, thanks to a special mechanism, while from appropriate flower-shaped holes in laminate of ivory, flower petals and perfumes showered down upon the guests.

Domus Aurea.
The Room of Achilles in Sciro.

◆ **FORO ROMANO** (Roman Forum).

The center of the civic and economic life in Republican times, the Forum maintained an important role also in the Imperial period. With the fall of the Roman Empire in the west, however, it went into decline. An earthquake in 851 during the papacy of Leo IV caused extensive damage, but the decisive blow was the devastating fury of the Normans who, although they came to Rome in 1084 ostensibly to help pope Gregory VII, sacked and set fire to the city.

The Forum was crossed by the **Via**

Gold coin with the profile of the Emperor Nero.

*The Roman Forum
as it was in
Imperial times
and as it is today*

Forum Romanum

1. Curia and Comitium
2. Arch of Septimius Severus
3. Rostra
4. Via Sacra
5. Temple of Saturn
6. Column of Phocas
7. Basilica Julia
8. Basilica Emilia
9. Temple of Julius Caesar
10. Temple of Vesta
11. Temple of Castor and Pollux
12. Arch of Augustus
13. Temple of Antoninus and Faustina
14. Temple of Romulus
15. Temple of Venus and Roma
16. House of the Vestal Virgins
17. Basilica of Maxentius
18. Colosseum
19. Arch of Titus
20. Palatine Hill

The Temple of Saturn.

The Temple of Antoninus and Faustina.

Sacra, which led to the Capitol Hill and also served as the route of the triumphal processions of victorious generals laden with booty and followed by ranks of prisoners. While the oldest section of the Forum (built in the Republican era) stretched from the opposite side of the valley to the edge of the Capitol Hill, the entrance on the square of the Colosseum leads to the most recently built section, which dates from the Imperial Age.

♦ On the Via Sacra, at the top of the Velia, is the **Arch of Titus**, which the Senate built after the Emperor's death in memory of his conquest of Jerusalem (70 A.D.). On the inside of the arch are two fine bas-reliefs: the Emperor on his triumphal chariot and the procession of the Jewish prisoners carrying a seven-branched candelabrum.

Model of the Basilica of Maxentius.

♦ The immense **Basilica of Maxentius** (also called the Basilica of Constantine) was the last edifice built in the city which conveys the magnificence of Ancient Rome. It was begun by Maxentius and completed by his successor Constantine. Part of this imposing 4th century structure has been restored, revealing the portion which faced the Forum and the smaller northern aisle. The great apse and powerful barrel vaults were a source of inspiration to Renaissance architects; it is thought that this ruin inspired Bramante's plans for the new St. Peter's.

♦ The **Temple of Antoninus and Faustina** is the best preserved building in the Forum. The loss of Faustina embittered her husband, the Emperor Antonius Pius. After her death, the Emperor wanted to deify her and built a magnificent temple in her honor (141 A.D.). This

The Temple of Vesta.

temple was transformed in the middle ages into the church of "San Lorenzo in Miranda". Many pagan temples were converted into Christian churches, including the ancient **Church of Sts. Cosmus and Damian**, built in 572 by Felix IV inside the "Templum Sacrae Urbis" which the Emperor Vespasian had constructed in the adjacent **Forum of Peace** (or "Vespasian's Forum").

The vestibule stands on the **Tempietto Rotondo**, or Round Temple of Romulus, son of Maxentius, and features its original bronze door and lock.

♦ The round **Temple of Vesta** dates from the time of King Numa Pompilius (8th century B.C.), when it was built to guard the Palladium (the image of Minerva) and other sacred objects brought to Italy by Aeneas, and upon which it was believed the security of the city depended. The six Vestals were chosen from patrician maidens, the daughters of free men, and had to keep the fire burning. They enjoyed special privileges, but if one broke her vow of chastity, she was buried alive in the Campo Scellerato (Field of Villains). They lived nearby in the **House of the Vestal Virgins**, which was almost totally reconstructed, along with the Temple of Vesta, by the Emperor Septimius Severus after a fire in 191 A.D. Many statues and interesting inscriptions remain. The house, comparable to a modern convent, was divided into different chambers which opened onto the large central atrium. Both the temple and the house of the Vestals once belonged to the first **Regia** of Rome, which according to tradition was the royal residence founded by the second king of Rome, Numa Pompilius, and later home to

Statue of the Emperor Marcus Aurelius (2nd century AD).

The powerful Corinthian columns of the Temple of Castor and Pollux "Dioscuri" erected in 484 AD.

The atrium of the House of the Vestal Virgins adorned by an enormous basin.

the "Pontifex Maximus" (highest priest). From the plan of the sacred building it is possible to recognize a trapezoidal part at the north end and a rectangle to the south, divided in three rooms.

♦ The **Temple of Julius Caesar**, which Octavian built in memory of his uncle, was begun in 42 B.C. on the spot where the dictator's body was burned, and consecrated in 29 A.D. together with the nearby **Arch of Augustus**, of which only the foundation remains.

♦ The **Temple of Castor and Pollux** (also called the "Temple of the Dioscuri") was built in 484 B.C. to commemorate the victory of Aulus Postumius over the Latins in the battle of Lake Regillus. The three Corinthian columns and part of the cornice date to the era of Tiberius or Hadrian (1st or 2nd century A.D.).

♦ **Santa Maria Antiqua** is one of the oldest Roman basilicas, resulting from a transformation of an Imperial edifice that had been annexed to the "Atrium Minervae" in the 5th century. The church consists of an atrium, courtyard (narthex), three naves and a presbytery. Frescoes in poor condition, dating from the 8th century, decorate the walls of the apse. The church was buried by a landslide in the ninth century, and only resurfaced after excavations in 1900.

♦ The **Basilica Julia**, built by Julius Caesar in the middle of the 1st century B.C., was an enormous structure with five naves , divided in sections with movable partitions, which allowed more than one audience to take place at the same time. Chess squares and other games traced into the marble on the steps of the building offer an interesting look at life in the Forum and the way in which Romans passed the time. After all the vicissitudes of the Forum, the vast basilica underwent a final restoration in 277 A.D.

♦ The **Column of Phocas** was the last classical monument added to the Forum. At the beginning of the 7th century, the Byzantine Emperor Phocas allowed Pope Boniface IV to convert the Pantheon into a Christian church. The column was erected in 608 A.D. by the representative of the Emperor in Rome, by taking a column and base from a pre-existing monument and mounting a bronze statue of the Byzantine Emperor on top.

♦ The **Temple of Saturn** was erected by the Consul Titus Larcius on the 17th of December, B.C. It was always used as the public treasury, and as a repository for the standards of the Legions and the decrees of the Senate. Sacred treasures were held in an underground chamber. The temple was enlarged in 42 B.C., and rebuilt after a fire in the 4th century A.D.

♦ Three columns remain of the **Temple of Vespasian** which was built by the son of Domitian in 94 A.D. and later restored by Septimius Severus.

♦ The **Temple of Concord** was built by Furio Camillo, the conqueror of the Gauls in 367 B.C. in memory of the agreement concluded at Monte Sacro between the plebians and patricians. It was in this temple that the Senate gathered to hear the last "Catilinaria" of Cicero (63 B.C.).

♦ The complex, overdone **Arch of Septimius Severus** points to the coming decline of Roman art. It had been erected in honor of Septimius and his sons, Caracalla and Geta. In the inscription recalls an Imperial tragedy: the murder of Geta by Caracalla, who later had his brother's name removed from the monument. Septimius Severus reigned for 18 years (193-211) and, quite unusually for the 3rd century, died of natural causes.

♦ The **Milarium aureum** is the column upon which were inscribed, in golden letters, the distances of the principal cities of the Roman Empire from Rome.

♦ The famous **Lapis Niger** was found during the excavations of 1899. The square area, paved in

Detail of the Arch of Septimius Severus.

Roman Forum. The broad foundation of the Basilica Giulia. To the left, the Colonna di Foca and the three columns of the Temple of Castor and Pollux. In the background stands the Palatine Hill and the remains of the Domus Tiberiana.

black marble, is the presumed location of the tomb of Romulus, the founder of Rome. The monument dates to the era of the Roman kings, and contains the oldest known inscription of a Latin epigraph.

◆ The **Comitium**, where the representatives of the people gathered for public discussions, had previously been the tribunal. The Comitium consisted of the *square*, where the popular assembly met, and the *Curia*, where the Senate deliberated. It was in the Comitium in the early days of the Republic that Brutus condemned his two sons to death for plotting the return of King Tarquinius. The great voices of the Roman Republic were once heard here. Cicero, the great orator, recited his second and third "Catilinaria," and it was here that the head of the great writer and philosopher was put on display after his assassination.

View of Roman Forum. On the left: remains of the Temple of Julius Caesar, the Temple of Vesta, the Domus Tiberiana at Palatinus and the Temple of Castor and Pollux.

◆ The **Rostra**, of which the great platform is still visible, were built by Caesar in 44 B.C., shortly before his death. From this platform the orators and political leaders addressed the people. In Republican times, the tribune, which had been originally built of wood, was situated near the Comitium. In 338 B.C., it was decorated with the prows of the ships captured in the battle of Anzio: from then on "Ad rostra!" became the cry of the Roman people to call a meeting.

Roman Forum.
Aerial view.

The three columns of the
Temple of Vespasian.

◆ The **Curia** was the Forum's first civic center, and consisted of the **Curia-Comitium** complex located between the Basilica Emilia and the Arch of Septimius Severus, which served as meeting place for the Senate, and later as a setting for sacred ceremonies and early gladiator shows. It was founded by King Tullius Ostillius, and underwent several transformations over the centuries. In 80 B.C. it was restructured by Sulla, and moved by Caesar to its current location. After a fire in 283 A.D., the Curia was rebuilt by Diocletian. In the middle ages, it was transformed into a church dedicated to St. Hadrian and finally, in the 1930's, it was restored to its original appearance.

◆ The **Basilica Emilia** was built by Emilio Lepidus and Fulvius Nobilius in 179 B.C., and subsequently rebuilt and restored many times under the care of the Aemelia family, until a fire at the beginning of the 5th century did irreparable damage. It was one of the greatest buildings in the Forum, used as many others of its kind for the administration and courts of the city. In front of the Basilica is a small round foundation of the shrine of the "Venus Cloacina" on the point where the Cloaca Maxima entered the Forum.

◆ Another historic Roman hill, the **PALATINE**, faces the Forum, preserving unforgettable memories in its luxuriant vegetation. The Palatine was the center of Rome in two distinct periods: that of the Roman Kings and of the Empire. During the repu-

A visit to the Palatine should include two worthwhile stops. The Palatine Museum displays archeological materials that bear witness to the millennial history of the Palatine Hill: from prehistory (10th century BC) to the Roman Empire. Especially interesting are the funerary objects, the reproduction of the huts from the time of Romulus and, on the second floor, the beautiful statuary. The Loggia Mattei, frescoed by the Peruzzi school, bears precious testimony to the Renaissance appearance of the Palatine.

Courtyard of the Domus Augustana

The Imperial Palaces.

blic the Palatine was home to patrician families: Quintus Hortensius, the celebrated orator who emulated Cicero, had a house here which later was acquired and enlarged by Augustus. As soon as Augustus became Emperor, he made his Imperial residence on the Palatine. Subsequently, Tiberius, Caligula, the Flavii and finally Septimius Severus built palaces here. The Palatine was the cradle of Rome. According to legend, it was on the Palatine that Romulus first traced the square outline of the city, and from then on served as the seat of the Roman Kings. Accordingly, the Palatine was the chosen residence of emperors from Caesar to Septimius Severus. The only exception being Nero; and though he built his great Domus Aurea (Golden House) elsewhere, he never inhabited it. From atop the Palatine, the wiew is unparalleled, for its complex of ruins, and the wisely adapted ornamentation and for the truly stupendous panorama.

♦ The *Clivus Palatinus* leads up to the Palatine, and the stairs on the right to the splendid **Villa Farnese**, with its 16th century Casina and Farnese Gardens, supported by the powerful arches of the **Domus Tiberiana**. From the terrace on the left, the steps lead down to the Palatine Area, where, among other venerable memories, there are ruins of the temple of **Magnus Mater** with the statue of a seated Cibele, found in the 3rd century B.C. and completely rebuilt after a great fire destroyed it in 111 B.C.

♦ On the eastern boundary of the area are the ruins of the **Temple of Victory** (early 3rd century B.C.). There are also ruins of the wall of "Roma Quadrata," some blocks of tufa thought to have belonged to the hut of Romulus and traces of the **Scalae Caci**, an early access to the Palatine. An early cistern (6th - 5th century B.C.) is located on the square.

♦ The nearby **House of Livia** is a typical example of a patrician house of the late Republican period which together with the **House of Augustus** and the **Temple of Apollo** formed the Augustean complex, the first Imperial complex on the on the Palatine. The murals, in the Pompeian

The Circus of Domitian.

Roman chariot.

style, are interesting despite their poor condition.

• To the right is the **Palace of the Flavii**, designed by Rabirius for the Emperor Domitian. It included a basilica, aula regia and lararium on the left; a peristyle in the center; and a triclinium on the right, which features remains of pavement and two nymphaea, one of which is in very good condition. Under the pavement there are traces of pre-existing structures. Attached to the palace was the **Domus Augustana**, where the Imperial court lived.

• The **Stadium of Domitian** (160 meters x 48 meters) is surrounded by fragments of porticoes, statues, fountains, and on one side, the large niche of the Imperial loggia.

• Nearby are the ruins of the **Palace** and the massive **Baths of Septimius Severus**, at the foot of which rose the Septizonium, an imposing building whose remains were demolished by Pope Sixtus V. From above these colossal ruins, the **Belvedere** offers a magnificent panorama.

The Domus Augustana overlooks its inner courtyards with a multitude of windows.

3 - Circo Massimo and Trastevere

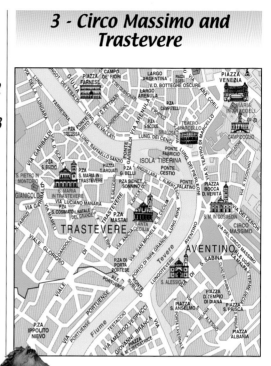

The Biga is a roman sculpture of the 1st century AD. Vatican Museums.

Circus Maximus 2000 years ago.

♦ At the foot of the hill, the enormous elliptical **Circus Maximus** (664 meters x 123 meters) runs along the base of the Palatiine Hill, almost entirely filling the space between the Palatine and Aventine Hills. The huge basin is still buried. Recent attempts to landscape the barren slopes have not been maintained. The structure was built in the time of the Etruscan kings, who transformed Rome from a village into a monumental city, on the place where religious rites and games in honor of the God Consus (the *Consualia*) were held since the times of Romulus. It was during this very celebration that the Rape of the Sabines occurred, to which the Romans resorted, according to the famous legend, in order to increase the population of the city. In the

time of Augustus, the Circus Maximus held 150,000 spectators, and with additions by Trajan, 250,000. The Circus was used for the Roman chariot races, which were among the greatest spectacles for the Roman people.

♦ To Piazza della Bocca della Verità, a site of great religious and commercial importance to pre-Roman settlers of the area, and later as the Roman **Forum Boarium** (cattle market).

♦ The 1ˢᵗ century B.C. temple named for **Fortuna Virile** is identified with the *Temple of Portunus*, the protector of the nearby port, and offers an excellent example of the Greco-

Model of the Circus Maximus overlooked by the Imperial Palaces of the Palatine Hill.

The Circus Maximus and the Imperial Palaces (below).

The Temple of Hercules Victor, kown as Temple of Vesta.

Reconstruction of the façade of the Marcellus Theater (1ˢᵗ century AD). It is the only ancient theater remained in Rome.

Italic architecture of the Republican era. In 872 A.D., a certain Stefano converted it into a Christian church dedicated to Santa Maria Egiziaca; it was then ceded to the Armenians.

♦ The church of **San Giorgio in Velabro** - named for the marsh (velabro) that once existed here - dates to the 7ᵗʰ century, though the lovely bell-tower and Ionic portico were added in the 12ᵗʰ century. A terrorist bombing in 1993 caused severe damage to the church, which was reopened in 1997 after extensive repairs and restoration.

♦ The **Arch of the Argentari**, a puzzling monument covered with poor reliefs, was built by money-changers and shop-keepers of the Forum Boarium and dedicated to Septimius Severus and Julia Domna, whose portraits are seen on the reliefs.

♦ Opposite is the entrance to the Cloaca Maxima, and the **Arch of Janus**, with four faces which date to the time of Constantine.

♦ **Santa Maria in Cosmedin**, one of the gems of medieval Rome, stands on the ruins of a *Temple to Hercules*, visible in the crypt of the church. The suggestive and austere interior is a good example of an early church (8ᵗʰ century). The elegant 12ᵗʰ century **campanile** (bell-tower) is in the Romanesque style. On the left side of the portico is a marble mask called the **Bocca della Verità** (Mouth of Truth): according to legend, a liar who puts his hand in the

mouth will have it bitten off. In Roman times the mask covered a drain hole nearby where the Cloaca Maxima flowed into the Tiber.

Roman columns with ancient capitals divide the interior of the church into three naves. The walls of the central nave are decorated with frescoes (8th - 12th century). The *baldacchino* (canopy) is in the Gothic style.

The Portico d'Ottavia. It originally sat within a dense network of colonnades. Augustus turned this area into a placed filled with monuments and recreational activities.

◆ Across from the church is the beautiful 2nd century B.C. **Round Temple**, the oldest Roman temple built of marble that exists today. In the past it was identified as a *temple to Vesta*, probably due to its resemblance to the temple of the same name in the Roman Forum. The latest archaeological evidence attributes it to **Hercules Victor**.

◆ The Jewish **Synagogue** was built in 1904 in the Babilonian style, with a gray aluminum cupola. Behind is the **Ghetto**, a neighborhood where the Jews of Rome were segregated from the 16th to the 19th century, and where many Jews still live.

◆ At the corner of Via Petroselli is the interesting medieval **Casa dei Crescenzi**, built in the 10th century for the powerful Crescenzi family, perhaps as a fort meant to guard the river. It is decorated with fragments from several Roman buildings.

The church of Saint Mary in Cosmedin with its beatiful romanesque bell tower. In the foreground the Triton fountain (1715).

◆ The fine **Theater of Marcellus** (recently restored) is the only ancient theater left in Rome. It was conceived by Julius Caesar and later built by Augustus in honor of Marcellus, son of his sister Octavia, who died in 23 B.C. at age 20, and was immortalized in the poetry of Virgil.

Model of the Isola Tiberina in Imperial era.

The original structure accommodated between 15,000 and 20,000 spectators.

What remains of the structure, which must have served as a model for the Colosseum, is a part of the curved exterior wall with an elegant double row of Doric and Ionic arches. Above is the 16th century Savelli palace (later of the Orsini) built into the theater by Baldassare Peruzzi.

To the right of Theater of Marcellus rise three columns from the *Temple of Apollo Sosiano* (5th century B.C.).

♦ Nearby are the remains of the **Portico di Ottavia** - built by Augustus to honor his sister. The propylaeum serves as the atrium of the 8th century church of **Sant'Angelo in Pescheria**, named for the fish market which was once located on the same site.

♦ A footbridge crosses from the Lungotevere to the **Isola Tiberina** (the island on the Tiber), where the church of **St. Bartholomew** stands on the ruins of the celebrated Temple of Aesculapius, the Greek God of medicine, once a pilgrimage site for the diseased.

♦ Two bridges join the island to the rest of the city: **Ponte**

The synagogue.

Aerial view of the Isola Tiberina.

Fabricius (also known as Quattro Capi), built in 62 B.C. and still intact today, and **Ponte Cestio** (46 B.C.). The nearby *Ponte Palatino Bridge* was formerly the site of the **Ponte Sublicio**, noted for the legend of Horace Cocles, the Roman hero who single-handedly fought the Etruscans under Porsenna.

♦ Crossing the *Palatine Bridge*, we come to **Trastevere**, the "heart of Rome", a quarter where popular traditions are still maintained despite the transformation connected with a certain internationalization of this celebrated part of the city. A detailed visit to this quarter, rich with old churches and fine buildings, cannot be included as a part of this book due to an obvious lack of space. Nevertheless, by finishing this itinerary with a stroll through the streets of Trastevere, one can get a good, authentic sense of the old city and perhaps find a typical restaurant, as well.

The Mouth of Truth *was a manhole cover of the famous Cloaca Massima.*

St. Mary in Trastevere with its Romanesque bell tower. In the foreground the fountain (15th cent.).

The Fontana Paolina, built by Flaminio Ponzio and Giovanni Fontana in the 17th century at the request of Pope Paul V.

♦ A brief note only about the oldest basilica in Rome, the church of **Santa Maria in Trastevere**, on the piazza of the same name. Founded by St. Calixtus in 221 and finished by St. Julius in 341, it was rebuilt in the 12th century by Pope Innocent II.

The **façade** was decorated, in the same period, with mosaics and frescoes, and then restored by Pietro Cavallini. In the 18th century, Pope Clement XI had Carlo Fontana build the portico, and Pope Pius IX had the basilica partly restored in 1870. Inside, the apse is decorated with marvelous mosaics, while between the windows are mosaics which portray the *story of the Virgin Mary* by Cavallini. Beside the facade is the lovely 12th century Romanesque campanile (bell tower) at the top of which is a niche with a mosaic representing a Madonna and Child.

♦ Following the panoramic Via Garibaldi we go up to the **Janiculum Hill**, which offers

some of the finest views of the city. Over the undulating sea of roofs, the numerous domes of Rome are silhouetted against the distant backdrop of the mountains, while the Tiber and its turns mark the city's unmistakable shape. On the great panoramic piazza is a **monument to Giuseppe Garibaldi** (1895) by Gallori.

♦ Ahead is the **Paoline Fountain**, built for Pope Paul V by G. Fontana in 1611. The huge semicircular basin was added in 1690 by Carlo Fontana.

♦ Down on the left is the church of **San Pietro in Montorio**. In the annex to the cloister beside the church, Bramante built a **Tempietto** over the supposed site of the crucifixion of St. Peter. The tiny temple is a masterpiece of the Italian renaissance, characterized by the wise use of classical elements such as columns and niches.

San Pietro in Montorio, Bramante's Tempietto.

The typical puppets on the Janiculum Hill.

The Janiculum hill with its wonderful panoramic view is linked to the name of the most ancient cult of Janus. It recalls above all the siege of Rome in 1849.

48

4 - From the Aventine to the EUR

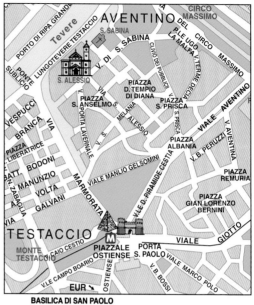

BASILICA DI SAN PAOLO

The municipal rose-garden at Aventino.

The ancient Church of Santa Sabina.

◆ In Imperial times, the **Aventine** was a patrician residential area. After the sacking by the Goths in 410 and the destruction of the splendid Roman villas, in the Christian era beautiful churches were built that still stand out against the lush green of the hill. Any visit to the Aventine should include a stroll in the **Orange Garden** (or Parco Savelli) surrounded by the crenellated walls of the 12th century Fortress.

Aerial view of the Pyramid, the tomb of Caius Cestius, the roman praetor and tribune. It stands beside the Porta San Paolo, one of the ancient gates to the city in the Aurelian Walls.

◆ After this green oasis we come to the ancient Church of **Santa Sabina** (432). The 12ᵗʰ century bell tower was lopped off in the 17ᵗʰ century; the interior underwent repeated refurbishment. Original features include: the *cypress doors of the middle portal* (5ᵗʰ century), with their panels representing the Old and New Testaments; the mosaic strip on the inside wall above the middle portal, with a metric inscription in gold letters against a blue background (5ᵗʰ century); the *frieze in opus sectile* running above and to the sides of the arches of the nave (also 5ᵗʰ century). Equally old are the *marble plutei*, used to restore the choir, with their fine, elegant, almost calligraphic reliefs.

◆ Just ahead is the Church of **Sant'Alessio**. Noted in the 7ᵗʰ century as a basilica connected to a monastery that may have been even older, it, too, underwent repeated refurbishing. It maintains a fine Romanesque *bell tower;* the crypt is also Romanesque, and unique in its kind in Rome.

◆ The **Pyramid of Caius Cestius**, at the end of Via Marmorata, was known in the middle ages as the *tomb of Romulus*. It was actually built in the last years of the Republic to house the ashes of Caius Cestius, who served as praetor, tribune and septemvir of the Epulos, as the two inscriptions attest.

A friar absorbed in prayer in the Orange Garden.

The basilica of St. Paul. Christ Pantocreator. Detail of the mosaic in the apse.

♦ About 2 kilometers down the Via Ostiense is the finest of the churches of Rome, the Basilica of **SAN PAOLO FUORI LE MURA** (St. Paul's Outside the Walls), built over the tomb of the "Apostle of the People." It was the Emperor Constantine who first built a church over St. Paul's tomb. A much larger basilica was built at the end of the 4th century; according to the mosaic inscription on the triumphal arch, it was begun by Theodosius, finished by Onorius, and restored and decorated by Placidias under Pope Leo I (440-461). This splendid basilica, one of the marvels of the world, was destroyed by fire in 1823. It was rebuilt by Pope Pius IX in 1854 on the same foundations according to the original design. The magnificent **four-sided portico**, consisting of 150 columns and a majestic statue of St. Paul at the center, immediately suggests a typical Roman basilica.

The mosaic **facade** glitters in gold and bright colors. In the portico, among other doors, is a *bronze door* by Antonio Maraini (1930). The inside of the basilica, split into five naves, is opulent and impressive; the eye seems to lose itself in the unending line of columns, among which a mystic light flows from the double row of

The Cosmatesque Cloister by Vassalletto.

alabaster windows. Above, the sumptuous
Renaissance-style *ceiling* in white and gold,
below, the shining marble pavement, and at the
end, under the triumphal arch, the lovely *baldacchino* (canopy) in front of the golden mosaics
in the apse. Between the windows and the
columns is a long series of *medallions* portraying
all the *popes* from St. Peter to Benedict XVI.

On the inner side of the facade, in addition to
the two columns which support the cornice, are
the *four alabaster columns* which supported the
enormous baldacchino by Poletti which covered
the ciborio (tabernacle) by Arnolfo di Cambio.
The mosaic on the **triumphal arch** dates to the
5th century, and was ordered by the Empress
Galla Placidia. It was placed here after a poor
restoration following the fire of 1823.

The Gothic style **canopy**, which stands on four
porphyry columns, is a 13th century masterpiece
by Arnolfo di Cambio. Under the papal altar is
the **marble arch** containing the glorious reliquary of St. Paul. On the right is Vassalletto's

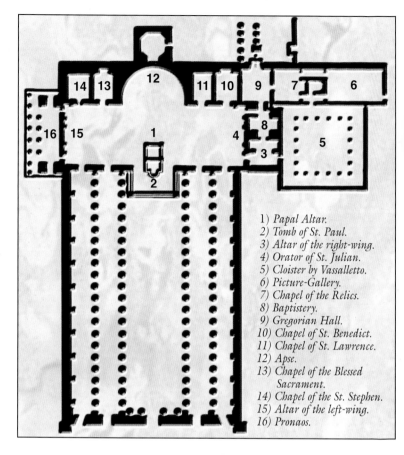

1) *Papal Altar.*
2) *Tomb of St. Paul.*
3) *Altar of the right-wing.*
4) *Orator of St. Julian.*
5) *Cloister by Vassalletto.*
6) *Picture-Gallery.*
7) *Chapel of the Relics.*
8) *Baptistery.*
9) *Gregorian Hall.*
10) *Chapel of St. Benedict.*
11) *Chapel of St. Lawrence.*
12) *Apse.*
13) *Chapel of the Blessed
     Sacrament.*
14) *Chapel of the St. Stephen.*
15) *Altar of the left-wing.*
16) *Pronaos.*

The interior of the Basilica of St. Paul.

Cosmatesque Cloister (restored in 1907), which is among the most significant examples of Roman marble work: a genuine masterpiece for its fine molding and the richness and elegance of its carvings and mosaics. The **facade** on Via Ostiense and the **bell-tower** are by Luigi Poletti (1850).

♦ Several kilometers further down the Via Ostiense is the **E.U.R.** quarter (named for the Esposizione Universale di Roma). Now largely residential, it was originally built to host the World Exposition of 1942, which did not take place

The Palazzo della Civiltà e del Lavoro is the Eur's most characteristic monument.

because of World War II. Although it has the typical features of fascist architecture, the quarter's urban plan is decisively more pleasant than other sprawling suburban developments which were built on the outskirts of Rome in the fifties and sixties. Worth noting, among other buildings, are the *Palazzo dei Congressi*; the *Palazzo della Civiltà e del Lavoro*; and the well-known *Palazzo dello Sport* (1960) by Pier Luigi Nervi, a brilliantly conceived structure from which extends a beautiful artificial *lake*.

Above, the lake in the Eur with, in the background, the Palazzo dello Sport built for the Olympic Games in 1960.

**Baths of
Caracalla, 54**

**Via Appia
Antica, 54 and 60**

Catacombs, 57

**Villa
dei Quintili, 60**

5 - Along the Via Appia Antica

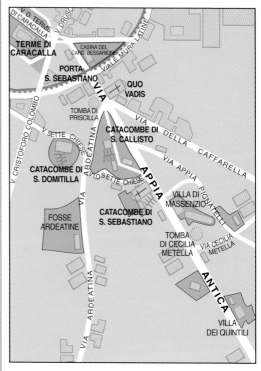

*This interesting figurative
capital is found in the
Baths of Caracalla.*

The Appian Way.

♦ More than any other road, VIA APPIA
ANTICA offers fascinating archeological and
artistic elements as well as lovely scenery. Proudly
called the "*regina viarum*" (queen of all roads),
it was begun by Appius Claudius in 312 B.C..
Tombs lined the sides of the road for miles, but
only members of patrician families, such as the
Scipios, Furii, Manili and Sestili were buried here.

♦ The first part of the Appian Way corresponds
today to *Via delle Terme di Caracalla* and *Via di
Porta San Sebastiano*. The first owes its name to
the famous **Baths of Caracalla**, or "*Antoniane*",
which were begun by Septimius Severus in 206
and opened in 217 by Caracalla, and were completed by their successors Heliogabalus and Alexander
Severus. Lined with basalt, granite and alabaster,
the enormous baths of hot, warm and cold water
could accommodate 1,600 at a time. Splendid
vaults, porticoes, esedrae and gymnasiums were
decorated with the most precious marble, the most
beautiful sculptures and the largest columns imagi-
nable. The ruins of this great complex are still
impressive for their size and majesty.

♦ On Via di Porta San Sebastiano, just near the fork in the road, is the **Casina del Cardinale Bessarione**, once home to the renowned humanist of Byzantine origin, who helped spread the cult of classical antiquity in Renaissance Rome. Built in the early 14ᵗʰ century, it was restored by the Cardinal in the middle of the 15ᵗʰ century. Illustrious humanists such as Flavio Biondo, Filelfo, Poggio, Campano, Platina gathered here around the great prelate for erudite discussions about art, science and especially Platonic philosophy. After the death of the Cardinal (1472), the house was abandoned and eventually reduced to a country restaurant. Careful restoration work in 1930 returned this precious architectural gem to its pristine grace.

Model of the Baths of Caracalla.

Aerial view of the baths of Caracalla. This is the best-preserved of the various bath complexes to be seen in Rome today.

Aerial view of the Porta San Sebastiano.

The façade of the Basilica of San Sebastiano by Vasanzio (1613).

♦ Nearby is the **Tomb of the Scipios**, which was discovered in the 17th century, and then abandoned until 1926, during which time the portions of greatest archaeological interest were removed. The monument was more complex than its name suggests: it is possible to visit - aside from the sepulcher of the famous family (used from the 3rd century B.C.) - a three story Roman house from the 4th century A.D. and Christian catacombs.

Just before the Porta di San Sebastiano, the road passes beneath the so-called **Arch of Drusus**.

♦ The **Porta di San Sebastiano** (once called the Porta Appia) leads out of the *Aurelian Walls*, begun by Aurelian in 271 and finished by Probus in 276. Still in excellent condition, they encircle a large part of Rome's historic center.

From here begins the most famous tract of the Appian Way, marked by particularly interesting stops, such as the chapel of the **Quo Vadis**, erected on the site where according to legend St. Peter had a vision of Christ. Nero's persecution of the Christians had driven St. Peter to abandon Rome, but a short way outside the city walls, he met another traveler who was walking quickly toward Rome. St. Peter recognized him: "Domine Quo Vadis?" (Oh lord, where are you going?). Jesus responded: "I'm going to Rome to be crucified a second time!"

♦ In front of the Chapel of the Quo Vadis is the circular ruin of the **Tomb of Priscilla**, beloved wife of Abascansius, a freed slave of the court of Domitian (81 - 96 A.D.) who died at a young age, and to whom the poet Cecilius Statius (1st century A.D.) dedicated a poem.

♦ As well as the vestiges of classical Rome, the Appian Way also offers some of the most important evidence about early Christianity. Some of the best-known Roman catacombs, as these ancient Christian subterranean cemeteries have been called since the 9th century, lie beneath the ancient road. The term **Catacomb** (from the Greek *katà cymba* = near the cavity) actually first referred specifically to the site of the **Catacombs of St. Sebastian**, which was a pozzolana quarry whose galleries were used for the first Christian cemetery.

The catacombs were greatly expanded with the spread of Christianity in Rome; cunicula

Detail of the statue of Saint Sebastian by Giorgetti (1672), done on a design by Gian Lorenzo Bernini.

The Catacombs of San Sebastiano. The Three Mausoleums.

Above, the Catacombs of San Callisto. The Crypt of St. Cecilia.

The Catacombs of San Callisto: the Crypt of the Popes.

were carved out on various levels for kilometers, resulting in an inextricable spider web in which it is easy to lose your way. For this reason visits to the catacombs are conducted by official guides from the Franciscan order, who are the caretakers of the cemetery complex. The Catacombs of St. Sebastian, above which a great basilica was built in the 4th century, were discovered during a 17th century restoration by Flaminio Ponzio and Giovanni Vasanzio. On the second level underground is the **Crypt of St. Sebastian**, where the body of the saint remained until it was transferred to the basilica during the restoration work. The *Cubiculum of Jonah*, with interesting frescoes of the biblical story of Jonah, and the scene of Noah saved from the Ark (late 4th century); the *Sarcophagus of Lot*; the *"Piazzola"*, an early entrance to the catacombs. The *Three Mausoleums* (in particularly good condition) face the Piazzola.

♦ The **Catacombs of St. Calixtus** were the first official burial place for the Christian community in Rome. All the popes of the 3rd century were buried here in the *Papal Crypt*. The first group of crypts was the *Cubiculum of St. Cecilia* (178 A.D.). The statue of the young martyr is by Maderno. After the Crypt of the Popes are the *Cubicula of the Sacraments*, the *Chapel of Pope Gaius*, and the *Crypt of St. Eusebius*.

♦ The **Catacombs of Domitilla** are named after the Christian lady to whom this land belonged. She was a member of the Flavians, an Imperial family. These are possibly the most extensive catacombs in Rome. In this area stands the 4th century *Basilica of Sts. Nereus and Achilleus*, which was discovered in 1874 and subsequently restored.

♦ Opposite the Catacombs of St. Sebastian is the **Villa of Maxentius**. Built in the early 4th century, it was immediately used as an imperial residence, but for only a few years. After the victory of Constantine over Maxentius (312 A.D.) and the transfer of the capital of the Empire to the "New Rome" at Constantinople, the Villa was ceded to the Christian church. Today it appears to be a large and well-exca-

The Catacombs of San Callisto. A hallway.

Roman Catacombs, detail of a fresco.

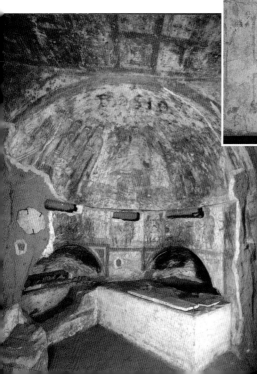

The Catacombs of Domitilla. Cubiculum of the Pistores.

The Villa dei Quintili.

Following page: interior of the Basilica of San Clemente with its dazzling apse decorated in mosaics, from the first half of the 12ᵗʰ century. In the center of the nave, the Schola Cantorum.

Of all the roads leading to Rome, the Appian Way was the queen, as the poet Statius called it.
Walking along it today is like taking a stroll through the history of Rome: from the most ancient vestiges (the tumulus of the Oratii and Curiatii) to the Christian catacombs and the modern villas hidden in the greenery. Since 2000, the Appian Way has featured a concentration of new service facilities between the third and fourth miles.

vated *archaeological site. Among the ruins is the Tomb of Romulus,* son of Maxentius, who died at a young age; the splendid, well-preserved Circus which once held 10,000 spectators; and finally, built over a country villa that dated to the 2ⁿᵈ century B.C., the *Imperial Palace* with three apses, two nymphea from the first imperial period, and a thermal complex.

♦ The **Tomb of Cecilia Metella** (circa 50 B.C.) stands solemnly on the Appian Way. Cecilia was the wife of Licinius Crassus, son of Crassus the triumvir, who ruled Rome along with Caesar and Pompey and put an end to the Republican era, making way for the Empire (1ˢᵗ century A.D.). The original commemorative marble tablet remains inside the tomb, which was transformed into a fortress in the middle ages. From here to the fourth mile, the Appian Way remains as it has been since the mid-19ᵗʰ century, when Luigi Canina redesigned it as a romantic road, lined by ancient tombs (mostly restored).

♦ Continuing to the fifth mile, after passing many monumental tombs, is the grand **Villa dei Quintili** (2ⁿᵈ century A.D.). It was once the country residence of the Quintilii brothers, Condianus and Maximus, who both served as Consuls, but was then confiscated by the Emperor Commodus, who transformed it into a lavish country palace. Though it was transformed into a fortress in the middle ages, the baths, a hippodrome, residences and gardens of the older structure are still visible.

Via Appia Antica.

6 - The Lateran and San Lorenzo

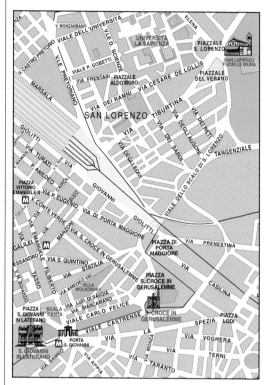

The Lateran Obelisk.

♦ The BASILICA DI SAN CLEMENTE, mentioned by St. Jerome in the 4th century, is among the most interesting churches in Rome from both an artistic and historical point of view. The church was almost buried among the ruins after a terrible fire set by the Normans during a siege in 1084. It was rebuilt in the 12th century by Pope Pasqual II directly above the original basilica, following the same plan, and using whatever architectural elements could be re-used. Despite more recent additions and restructuring, San Clemente remains a rare example of a paleo-Christian basilica. It was not possible to preserve the exact dimensions of the lower church, because the foundations of the right nave had been too severely damaged to allow construction above that area. In fact, in the external wall of the *upper church* are inserted the arches of the colonnade (still visible from the wall near the sacristy) that in the lower basilica had been used to divide the right nave from the large central nave. Consequently, the

San Clemente. The Crucifix with the twelve doves. *Detail of the apse mosaic.*

central and right nave in the upper basilica had to be narrowed, leaving the left nave as the only portion which directly corresponds to the lower basilica.

The three naves are separated by two rows of columns, each interrupted by a pilaster. The columns - each different from the others - were probably retrieved from the remains of buildings destroyed by the fire mentioned above. The most characteristic elements of the upper basilica are the *protiro* (or entry portico) and, inside, the enclosure known as the "*schola cantorum*", which belonged to the earlier basilica, while the ambones and the twisted candelstick date to the 12th century.

The tabernacle and Episcopal chair, at the center of the typical semicircular bench used only by the clergy which runs along the apse,

San Clemente.
Detail of the apse mosaic depicting The Tree of Life.

Interior of the Basilica of San Clemente.

The Sancta Sanctorum.
The Scala Santa.

also date from the same period.

The highlight of the basilica is the **apse mosaic**, which represents, in a prodigious synthesis of pagan and Christian figurative elements, the **scene of the Redemption**, a masterpiece of the Roman school of the 12th century.

The *lower basilica*, discovered as a result of excavations in the 19th century, along with other Republican and Imperial structures underneath (among them a Mithraic temple) make this a fascinating archaeological site.

The basilica also features several masterpieces of renaissance art. In the first chapel of the left nave are celebrated *frescoes* by Masolino da Panicale (1431) - once attributed to Masaccio: to the left of the entrance is **St. Christopher**; on the central wall a dramatic **Crucifixion scene**; on the right side wall, episodes from the life of **St. Ambrogio**; on the left side wall, the martyrdom of **St. Catherine** of Alexandria; on the altar, a **Madonna** by Sassoferrato.

◆ On Piazza di San Giovanni in Laterano rises the red granite **Lateran Obelisk**, the tallest of the obelisks which stand today on various piazzas in Rome. It was made in 1449 B.C. by Totmes III and his son Totmes IV of the 18th dynasty of the Pharaohs and brought to Rome

St. John Lateran. The interior of the Baptistry.

in the 4th century, where it was erected on the Circus Maximus. It was then moved here by Fontana for Pope Sixtus V in 1588.

• The LATERAN was the residence of the popes until 1309, when the papacy was transferred to Avignon. The palace, called the Patriarchium, was pulled down in 1586 by Domenico Fontana on orders from Pope Sixtus V, who ordered the construction of the current building.

• The **Baptistery**, on the piazza, was built by Constantine on the spot once thought to be the site of his baptism by St. Sylvester. It was then rebuilt by Pope Sixtus III (432-440) and subsequently restored several times. Eight porphyry columns which support the cornice of the octagonal structure, while another eight marble columns support the cupola.

• On the opposite side of the piazza is the building containing the SCALA SANTA (Holy Staircase), thought to be the same flight of steps which Jesus ascended in the house of Pontius Pilate; it was brought to Rome by the Empress Helena. The staircase has twenty-eight marble steps, recovered with wood for protection, while small glass sheets cover some spots that are considered to be a trail of Christ's blood. Both the Holy Staircase that the Christians climb on their knees and the four lateral stairs end in front of one of the most venerable monuments of history and art of the Medieval Ages, the SANCTA SANCTORUM, or *Chapel of St. Lawrence*, come to us with the changes made under Pope Nicholas III in the last years of the 13th century. It retains numerous important features of decorative art, mostly the splendid mosaic flooring and frescoes

The Scala Santa.

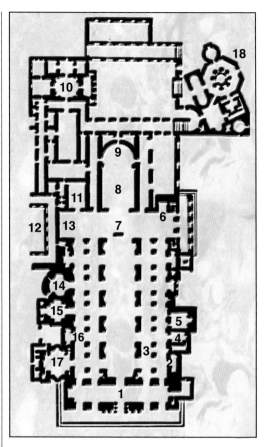

Pope Boniface VIII inaugurates the first Holy Year in 1300, in a fresco by Giotto.

of the school of the major painters of the 13th century, Cimabue of Florence and the Roman Pietro Cavallini. Thanks to these basic works of art, this Chapel has been called "the Sistine of the Medieval Age"; but the attention and the emotions of the visitor concentrate mostly in the famous *table of the Redeemer*, a precious icon that has been dated to the 6th century.

♦ SAN GIOVANNI IN LATERANO (Saint John Lateran), the Cathedral of Rome, was founded by Constantine as the Basilica of the Savior, during the papacy of St. Sylvester (314-335). It was destroyed and rebuilt several times; the current basilica dates to the 17th century. The imposing facade in travertine was built in 1735 by the architect Alessandro Galilei. The balustrade above the attic

The Basilica of St. John Lateran.

holds 15 statues which represent Christ, St. John the Baptist and the Doctors of the Church. In the left side of the portico is a *statue of Constantine* brought from the Imperial Baths at the Quirinal; the *bronze doors* were taken from the Curia in the Roman Forum by Pope Alexander VII (1655-1667).

The last door on the right is the **Holy Door**, opened only during holy years. The reliefs on the door, with episodes of the life of St. John the Baptist, are the work of different 18th century sculptors.

The **inside** of the basilica, 130 meters long, is divided in five naves by ancient columns which Borromini skillfully incorporated into gigantic *pilasters* in the mid-17th century. In the pilasters he placed a series of statues of the apostles, set into niches framed by green marble columns, thus creating a splendid chromatic contrast of green, gray and white. Above the niches are *high reliefs in stucco* by Algardi (1650), representing *scenes from the Old and New Testaments.*

The most striking parts of the interior are the sumptuous gilded *ceiling* in the central nave by Pirro Ligorio (1562) and the *Cosmatesque floor,* under which notable ruins from the Roman period were found.

On the sides of the aisle, prominent niches made of ancient green marble were set into the

The papal altar surmounts the confession, in which rises the statue of St. John the Baptist.

The interior of the Basilica. The papal altar under the canopy was erected by Pope Urban V in 1367.

St. John. The tabernacle.

rows of pillars by Borromini, into which the colossal *statues of the Twelve Apostles*, sculpted in the Bernini school during the first twenty years of the 18th century, have been placed. The twelve ovals painted among the windows, corresponding to the twelve Prophets, also belong to the 18th century.

The vastness of the central nave has as a background an imposing *tabernacle* (late 14th century), decorated by twelve small frescoes attributed to Barna da Siena. The Good Shepherd, the Crucifixion, the Blessed Virgin, and numerous Saints are represented. Above, the *relics of the heads of Sts. Peter and Paul* are kept in precious silver containers.

Under the tabernacle is the *papal altar* - used only by the pope - made

under Pope Urban V in 1367 and restored in 1851. On a bronze *slab* in the crypt is the splendid work of Simone Ghini (1443), brother of Donatello, who *sculpted the prostrate Pope Martin V* with the inscription "temporum suorum felicitas" (the happiness of his times).

The *presbyterium* and the *apse*, at the end of the basilica, are the result of a project carried out by Francesco Vespignani (1884-86) for Pope Leo XIII. Ordered to extend the apse, the artist moved and restored the *Mosaic of the Redeemer*, which dates to the initial construction of the basilica (4th century), and had been restored almost a thousand years later by Jacopo Torriti and Jacopo da Camerino, in 1291. Below, the *papal throne* is made of pre-

St. John. The canopy.

Basilica of San Giovanni. The cloister, a masterpiece of Cosmati art, built by Vassalletto between 1215 and 1232.

cious marble and studded with dazzling mosaics. In the left transept is the *Altar of the Sacrament*, designed by Olivieri (1592-1604); the four bronze columns had probably been brought from the Campidoglio by Constantine.

Also on the left is a door that leads to the large *Cloister*, a glorious masterpiece of 13th century Cosmatesque art. It was the work of the most famous Roman marble artisans, the Vassalletto family, who were also responsible for the cloister of the Basilica of St. Paul.

◆ Not far off rises the Basilica of the HOLY CROSS IN JERUSALEM (or *Sessoriana* or *Eleniana Basilica*). It is thought to have been built, or rather, to have been adapted from the Sessorian palace, in the beginning of the 4th century, by the mother of Constantine, St. Helena,

The Lateran.

who placed a *Relic of the Holy Cross* there together with others found by her at Jerusalem. It has often been restored and in 1743 it was almost entirely rebuilt by order of Benedict XIV. The facade, standing in the centre of the plain walls of the Cistercian monastery, is characterized by a curved and sinuous outline.

The *atrium* is particularly original, built to an oval design with the entrance on the lesser curve and covered by a dome which is also oval. The 13th century bell tower is still standing. The interior has a nave and two aisles. In the apse is a fresco by Antoniazzo Romano, the *Discovery of the Holy Cross*. The *Chapel of Relics* is the work of the architect Di Fausto (1930). In the crypt is a marvellous mosaic by Melozzo da Forlì. The *Statue of St. Helena*, except for the head and the hands, is a reproduction of the *Juno Vaticana*.

♦ Nearby rises the **Porta Maggiore**, more imposing than all the gates of Rome. It is a monumental arch with two vaults constructed at the time of Claudius. The inscription records the construction of Claudius' aqueduct and the restorations by Vespasian and Titus.

Santa Croce in Gerusalemme. The valuable work by Valadier with the reliquaries of Christ's Cross.

Santa Croce in Gerusalemme. The central nave.

The façade of Santa Croce in Gerusalemme.

The interior of the Basilica of San Lorenzo.

◆ The fifth patriarchal basilica **SAN LORENZO FUORI LE MURA** (Saint Lawrence outside the walls), was originally erected by Constantine; after the sack by Alaric and the Goths, Pelagius II rebuilt it during 579-590. The Longobards damaged it further, and Hadrian I (722-795), or according to others, Honorius III (1216-26) restored it in such a way that the old Constantinian part of the basilica became the presbitery of the new one; the original entrance was on the opposite side.

In the 13th century portico by Vassalletto there are six Ionic columns; two Roman Lions flank the portal. On the right, a block of stone commemorates the unfortunate bombardment of July 19th, 1943, after which a large part of the Basilica had to be rebuilt. The restoration, which was completed in 1949, left the three aisles their original design. Opposite, the funeral *Monument in memory of Alcide De Gaspari*, a great Italian politician statesman who died in 1954, extremely valuable work by Giacomo Manzú.

The interior is neat and severe, divided into three naves by twenty-two granite and cipolino columns taken from the ancient Roman monuments. The pavement, the two ambones, and the candlestick for the Easter candle are Cosmatesque masterpieces.

On the right of the central door of the church is a Roman sarcophagus decorated with a finely carved scene of a nuptial ceremony. It was adapted as a *Tomb for Cardinal Fieschi*, nephew of Innocent IV, who died in 1256. The two large amboes are of the Cosmati epoch.

In the middle, on the High Altar, there is the valuable *ciborium*, made by a famouse family of Roman marble workers, Paolo and sons, who signed and dated it in 1148.

The *floor* is also cosmatesque. A large hole opened by the bombardment uncovered traces of the apse of the Basilica of Constantine's time.

San Lorenzo fuori le Mura. The ciborium.

The Basilica of San Lorenzo fuori le Mura.

7 - Quirinal and Esquilino

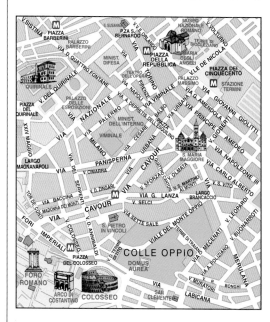

*Cuirassier in full
uniform.*

The Quirinal Palace.

♦ The immense QUIRINAL PALACE was begun by Pope Gregory XII in 1574, and served as a residence to the popes until 1870, then to the king of Italy after the declaration of Rome as the nation's capital, and finally to the President of the Republic since 1946. The palace is open to the public on occasion, and inside are works by Bernini, Guido Reni, Maderno and Giulio Romano.

◆ At the center of the piazza is a beautiful *fountain* made from a granite basin taken from the Roman Forum and brought here in 1818 by Raffaele Stern, along with an *obelisk* from the Mausoleum of Augustus and the imposing *statues of Castor and Pollux.*

◆ On the right, the elegant and majestic **Palazzo della Consulta**, by Fuga (1732-34).

◆ Down Via del Quirinale is the church of **Sant'Andrea al Quirinale** (1658), a favorite work by Bernini and further down, **San Carlino** by Borromini: a tiny church and cloister, both full of grace and elegance. Just ahead is the intersection called the *Quattro Fontane* (Four Fountains), with the quadruple background of Porta Pia and the three obelisks on the Esquiline, Quirinal and Pincian hills.

◆ Piazza della Repubblica occupies what was once an esedra of the Baths of Diocletian. At the center of the piazza is the **Fountain of the Naiads**, by Mario Rutelli (1900).

◆ The entire area is dominated by the colossal complex of the BATHS OF DIOCLETIAN, which once extended for over thirteen

The Fountain of the Naiads by Mario Rutelli was inaugurated in 1901 and created a furor because of the excessively realistic sensuality of the four nude bronze nymphs. In the center, the sea god Glaucus, defeating the hostile forces of nature.

The Palazzo della Consulta on the Piazza del Quirinale. To the right, two cuirassiers on horseback.

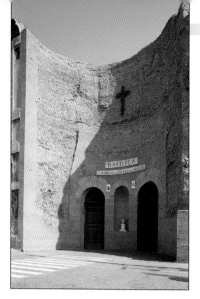

The façade of the Basilica of Santa Maria degli Angeli. This formed the exedra of the calidarium at the Baths of Diocletian.

Aerial view of the Baths of Diocletian, with the Basilica of Santa Maria degli Angeli, carved out of a portion of the enormous complex.

hectares - far larger than the majestic structure that stands today between Piazza del Cinquecento and Piazza della Repubblica.

♦ The original plan of the baths can also clearly be seen in the Church of SANTA MARIA DEGLI ANGELI E DEI MARTIRI (St. Mary of the Angels and of the Martyrs) which Michelangelo built within the Roman complex respecting all the characteristics of his concepts and genius. The entrance into the basilica was to open in the direction of the present day Piazza dei Cinquecento, where the National Roman Museum is presently located, but in the 1700's, Luigi Vanvitelli altered the original project.

Its present **entrance** was opened, formed by the façade of the calidarium of the baths. This change drastically reduced the impression of grandiosity obtained by Michelangelo thanks to the exceptional vastness of the entrance area he had originally chosen.

The present **atrium** corresponds to the tepidarium of the baths. Its sober decorations faithfully preserve its original nature. The central part of the church, in the shape of a Greek cross favoured by Buonarroti, corresponds to the central hall of the baths.

The **transversal nave**, which corresponds to

Michelangelo's central nave, contains eight beautiful monolithic columns in red granite, each one spectacular in size: 5 meters in circumference, 14 meters in height (taller than a four-story building). Originally each column measured 16 meters in height, but Michelangelo was forced to raise the pavement by 2 meters in order to protect the church from the humidity.

During the middle of the 1700's, Luigi Vanvitelli added the same amount of columns that were an imitation of granite and each with stucco capitals. The **apse** is also by Vanvitelli who cut into two halves the large pool or swimming area which had remained intact until then.

◆ Behind the neighbouring Piazza dei Cinquecento, is the modern façade of the main railway station, **Stazione Termini**, which was finished in 1950.

◆ Founded in 1889, the **MUSEO NAZIONALE ROMANO** sits across a large piazza from Stazione Termini in what was once the Certosa of Santa Maria degli Angeli and the Baths of Diocletian, a stunning setting for one of the most precious archaeological collections in the world, made up of priceless relics found in Rome and Lazio in the last decades of the 19th century. The constant flow of archaeological finds necessitated the expansion of the museum, and two separate buildings, the nearby Palazzo Massimo alle Terme and

The façade of the Basilica of Santa Maria degli Angeli, the Baths of Diocletian, and, in the center of the Piazza della Repubblica, the Fountain of the Naiads.

The large number of works collected by the Museo Nazionale Romano led the Italian government to purchase new exhibition sites to supplement the traditional Baths of Diocletian. These include the nearby Palazzo Massimo alle Terme, with its entrance on Largo di Villa Peretti, and Palazzo Altemps in Piazza Sant'Apollinare, near Piazza Navona.

Palazzo Altemps (at Piazza Sant'Apollinare, near Piazza Navona, see p. 108) have been recently renovated to hold a major portion of the collection.

After a long restoration, visitors to the Baths of Diocletian can explore the three floors of the epigraphy section, with priceless historic finds, as well as the galleries of the section devoted to the Latin peoples, and Michelangelo's cloister.

The renovation of the baths did not alter the Great Cloister or **Cloister of Michelangelo**, attributed to the inimitable artist. Square in form, it is enclosed by a portico formed by one hundred arcades and one hundred columns. One of the most sumptuous cloisters in Rome, its walkways and central garden are richly adorned with statues and epigraphs.

◆ At a separate site on Piazza della Repubblica, the **Aula Ottagona** (formerly the Planetarium), is home to sculpture from these baths and other complexes, including a copy of a Praxiteles masterpiece from the 2nd century AD, the *Lyceum Apollo*, the *Hellenistic Prince*, and the realistic *Resting Boxer*, both bronzes from the 2nd century BC.

There are some depictions of Aphrodite (Venus), like the famous *Venus of Cyrene*, a 2nd century copy of a Late Hellenistic model.

◆ **PALAZZO MASSIMO ALLE TERME** was built in 1887 by the architect Camillo Pistrucci for the Jesuit Massimiliano Massimo, and served as the seat for the College of Jesuits until 1960. In 1981, the Italian Government acquired the building and restored it as the second seat of the Museo Nazionale Romano. Dedicated to ancient art, Palazzo Massimo holds in its three floors the most significant works produced between the end of the Republican period (2nd-1st century BC) and the late-Imperial period (4th century AD), in addition to a few Greek works from the 5th century BC. It offers a complete picture of the political and economic life of ancient Rome.

The Lancellotti Discus Thrower *(2nd century AD). Museo Nazionale Romano - Palazzo Massimo.*

Hellenistic Prince *(2nd century AD). Octagonal hall.*

Roman National Museum of Palazzo Massimo

The display on the ground floor is arranged in three galleries and eight rooms around a central courtyard. In the First Gallery are ten portraits from the late-Republican period. In the First Room, the visitor's attention is drawn to the marble statue of the so-called *General of Tivoli* (70 BC), found at Tivoli in the temple of Hercules Victor. In the Fifth Room is the *Augustus of Via Labicana*, in which the emperor appears in the clothing of the Pontifex Maximus, the saviour of the homeland. Several of the Greek sculptures in the Seventh Room come from the area of *Sallust's Gardens* (Rome's Ludovisi neighbourhood), once owned by the roman historian Sallust, and before that by Julius Caesar. The masterpiece of the room is the *Niobide* (440 BC). It represents a daughter of Niobe in the act of pulling an arrow out of her back, which Diana had shot. In the Eighth Room are copies of works by Greek sculptors made for Roman political figures who wanted to possess Greek works.

The first floor contains two galleries and fourteen rooms, some containing portraits, reliefs and sarcophagi which are examples of the official ichnography of Roman art from the 1st to the 4th century AD. In the remaining rooms are pieces representing the rich bronze and marble statue production inspired by Greek sculpture of the 5th to 4th century BC. In the Fifth Room, for example, there are works which come from villas in Rome and Lazio, among them Hadrian's Villa and the Villas of Nero at Anzio and Subiaco.

The Sixth Room contains the notable *Apollo of the Tevere*, attributed to Fidia and found in the bottom of the river; two other noteworthy statues are the *Discobolo Lancellotti* and the *Discobolo di Castelporziano*.

In the Seventh Room is the large *statue of Dionysius*, a bronze work from Hadrian's period (2nd century AD) and a beautiful sculpture of the *Sleeping Hermaphrodite*, a copy of a Greek original (both from the 2nd century BC).

In the Second Gallery are fine feminine statue-portraits that date to the 3rd and 4th century AD: *Giulia Domna*, wife of Septimius Severus, *Plautilla*, wife of Caracalla, and *Salonina*, wife of Gallieno.

The second floor holds *pictures, mosaics* and *stuccoes*, which demonstrate the luxury with which the villas and noble houses were decorated in Ancient Rome. Among the works are paintings of a garden from the Villa of Livia (wife of the Emperor Augustus) on the Via Flaminia; floor mosaics from the 2nd and 4th century AD; frescoes from the Villa of the Farnesina, along the Tiber, painted for the marriage of Agrippa and Julia in 19 AD; other mosaics, made of glass, shells and pumice, from the Nymphaeum of Anzio (1st and 2nd century AD) in the Villa of Nero; and floors from the Villa of Baccano on the Via Cassia (3rd century AD), which was probably owned by the Severi family.

Statue of Niobides.
Museo Nazionale Romano - Palazzo Massimo.

MAP OF THE BASILICA OF ST. MARY MAJOR

1) *Atrio.*
2) *Nave.*
3) *Baptistery.*
4) *Sistine Chapel.*
5) *Blessed Sacrament.*
6) *The Confession.*
7) *Canopy.*
8) *Apse.*
9) *Pauline Chapel.*
10) *Sforza Chapel.*
11) *Cesi Chapel.*

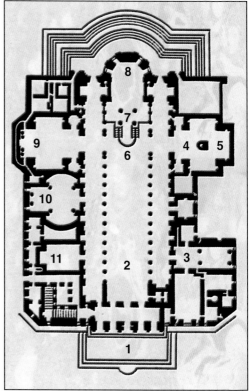

The Basilica of Santa Maria Maggiore. The apse mosaic by Jacopo Torriti (13th century).

Detail of the apse mosaic (lower section). Mary lying across the coffin.

♦ The Basilica of **SANTA MARIA MAGGIORE** is the fourth largest church in Rome and the largest dedicated to the Virgin Mary, and apart from some decorations, is the only basilica which still retains its original shape and character. In August of 356, the Virgin appeared in a dream before Pope Liberius and commanded him to build a church on the site where it would snow the following day. The legend is represented in the medieval mosaics (much restored) in the loggia of the portico. The Basilica, also called "Liberiana", was built in the time of Pope Sixtus III (432-440). The beautiful **façade**, by Fuga, features a portico

with five openings divided by pilasters decorated with columns, and a loggia with three great arches.

The Romanesque **campanile** (bell-tower) is the tallest in Rome.

The **interior**, with three naves, is a magnificent sight. At the end of a double row of columns, under the triumphal arch, is the great *baldacchino* (also by Fuga), supported by four splendid porphyry columns. The *ceiling*, by Giuliano Sangallo, was gilded with the first gold brought from America. Along the walls of the architrave, a series of thirty-six mosaics represent *scenes from the Old Testament*, which join the great mosaic of the *triumphal arch*, with scenes from the New Testament. All these mosaics, which date to the 5th century, are of particular importance and beauty. The *pavement* of the basilica is a fine Cosmatesque work of the 12th century. The *sarcophagus* in front of the high altar was decorated in 1874 by Vespignani, who used the rarest and most precious marble. Behind the metal grill are the celebrated relics of the *Presepio* (crib), consisting of five pieces of the manger in which Christ was put at birth, closed in a silver urn

The façade of the Basilica of Santa Maria Maggiore.

The alter canopy by Ferdinando Fuga (18th century).

Santa Maria Maggiore, the Chapel of the Holiest Sacrament, also called the Sistine Chapel.

The Basilica of Santa Maria Maggiore during a religious service.

designed by Valadier. In front is the large kneeling *statue of Pope Pius IX* by Jacometti (1880). On the *high altar*, under the great canopy, a sarcophagus contains the bones of *St. Matthew the Evangelist*. In the apse with the lancet windows is a fine mosaic of the *Triumph of Mary* by Torriti (1295). After having admired the entire mosaic cycle, let's return to the entrance in order to start an orderly tour of the side naves and the transept. On the right aisle, there is first of all the **Chapel of the Baptistry**, by Flaminio Ponzio (1605), while the porphyry Baptismal font is an 19th century work by Luigi Valadier. From the Baptistry, we walk to the adjacent sacristy by Flaminio Ponzio, where another two chapels stand out. The second Chapel in the right nave, the **Chapel of the Relics**, was built by Ferdinando Fuga (who also designed the façadeand of the canopy). The grandiose **Sistine Chapel** in the right wing of the transept was designed by the architect Domenico Fontana in the second half of the 16th century for Pope Sixtus V, who had expressed a desire to be buried here. The chapel was dedicated in the name of the pope, who com-

pletely changed the urbanistic aspect of Rome. Since the return of the popes from the Avignonese exile two centuries earlier, the city had been enriched and embellished considerably by beautiful churches and grandiose buildings, but it had retained its web of medieval streets. Thanks to the work of Domenico Fontana, Sixtus V changed the aspect of the city and earned himself a place in the history.

The architect therefore dedicated this Greek-cross shaped Chapel, surmounted by a frescoed dome, with a High Altar and a late 16th century ciborium in the shape of a small temple. Both the monument in memory of Sixtus

V and that of St. Pius V, the Pope under whom the Lepanto war (1571) was fought, were built by Domenico Fontana. After walking through the main aisle to the Confession, we can cross to the left wing of the transept and the symmetrical counterpart to the Sistine Chapel, the **Paolina Chapel**, named after Pope Paul V, who is buried there. It was built by the architect Flaminio Ponzio.

In front of the *Tomb of Paul V* (1605-1624), there is the *Tomb of Clement VIII Aldobrandini*

Santa Maria Maggiore, the Pauline Chapel with the altar to the Virgin by P. Targoni (1600).

Aerial view of the Basilica of Santa Maria Maggiore.

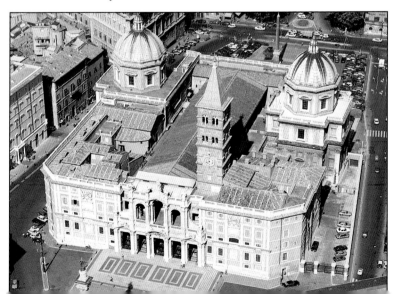

Basilica of St. Peter in Chains.
The statue of Moses.

Basilica of St. Peter in Chains. The chains that imprisoned St. Peter.

(1592-1605), his predecessor (between the two of them there was the very brief pontificate of the Medici Pope Leo XI, of the famous Florentine family, which lasted only a few mouths). Both the monuments were planned by the Architect of the Chapel, Flaminio Ponzio, who gave his masterpiece a character of splendid sumptuousness. The Chapels that face the left nave, although less rich, are also worthy of interest: although attributed to Giacomo Della Porta (1565-1573), the noble, organic design of the Sforza Chapel corroborates the hypothesis that it was designed by Michelangelo, as were many other works by that architect. In front of the church rises the beautiful **Corinthian Column** erected by Pope Paul V, who had it brought from the Basilica of Maxentius in the Roman Forum in 1615.

♦ The church of SAN PIETRO IN VINCOLI (St. Peter in Chains) was built under the generosity of an Imperial matron, Eudoxia, daughter of Theodosius the Younger and wife of the Emperor Valentinian III. The chains used by Herod to hold Peter were sent to Eudoxia by her mother, who had received them from the bishop of Jerusalem. To house the chains, the young Eudoxia built the basilica which was called "Eudoxiana," or more commonly "San Pietro in Vincoli."

The façade is of considerable interest. The elegant **portico** was built by an architect at the end of the 15th century for

Cardinal Giuliano della Rovere, the future Pope Julius II. He ordered Michelangelo to build him a funeral monument, and the first statue by the artist, the **Moses**, is the masterpiece that draws most tourists to the basilica. The statue was to be the central figure of an enormous mausoleum which was to have included forty statues. The tomb was instead erected in the right transept under Pope Paul III (1534-49) with only a few statues completed. Even if the monument falls short of Michelangelo's superb design, the potent sculpture of the biblical prophet is nonetheless among the most moving images of western art. The strong and secure Moses is portrayed in a very simple position, yet emanates a sense of majesty and strength that suggests divine investiture. The two *statues of Rachael and Leah* were also designed by Michelangelo. The church interior is imposing, the central nave is lined with twenty columns of antique marble. Among the many objects of art in the basilica are the *Tombs of Antonio Pollaiolo* (1432-1498), sculptor, jeweler, painter and engraver, and his brother *Piero*, by Luigi Capponi. The first altar in the right nave is Guercino's masterpiece *Sant'Agostino*. Finally, the 19th century gilded **bronze urn** in the reliquary under the high altar, which holds the **Chains of St. Peter**. Also deeply venerated are the *relics of the seven Macabee brothers*, held in a paleo Christian sarcophagus decorated with episodes from the New Testament, in the crypt.

The latest major restoration work on the funerary monument of Pope Julius II brought to light an unexpected find. It had always been believed that the Moses and the other works placed on the same level were by Michelangelo, whereas the sculptures placed on the upper level, including the splendid figure of Julius II at rest, were the work of lesser artists. In fact, the analogies with other sculptures by Michelangelo, the precise shaping, and other key figurative and stylistic elements in the statue of Julius II make it likely that it can be attributed to the great Master.

The interior of the Basilica of St. Peter in Chains.

8 - Via Veneto and Villa Borghese

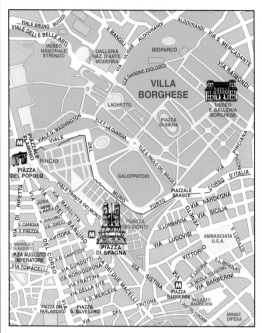

The Temple of Aesculapius on an island in the ornamental lake of the Villa Borghese gardens.

The fountain of the Triton at Piazza Barberini.

♦ We start from **Piazza Barberini** and Bernini's famous **Fountain of the Triton** (1643) and diagonally across the piazza is another Bernini fountain, the graceful **Fountain of the Bees**, and the beginning of the famous VIA VENETO.

Just ahead is the church of Santa Maria della Concezione, also known as the Church of Cappuccini, with a painting of **St. Michael** by Guido Reni and the **Ecstasy of St. Francis** by Domenichino. Beneath the church is the

National Gallery of Ancient Art
Palazzo Barberini

Down Via delle Quattro Fontane is the famous **Palazzo Barberini**, begun under Pope Urban VIII on designs by Maderno and continued by Borromini and Bernini in 1640. It houses the recently restored **Galleria Nazionale d'Arte Antica**.

Among the many paintings on display, which range from the 13th to the 16th centuries, there are several famous the world over: Raphael's **La Fornarina**, Tintoretto's **Christ and the Adultress**, Caravaggio's **Narcissus** and **Judith cutting the head of Holofernes**. The vault of the great hall of the palace was decorated with **The Triumph of Divine Providence** (1638) by Pietro da Cortona.

macabre **Cemetery of the Cappuccini**, which contains the bones of nearly 4000 friars.

♦ At the top of Via Veneto, past Porta Pinciana, we enter one of the most beautiful parks in the city, **Villa Borghese**. Immediately after the election of Paolo V Borghese as pope, his young nephew Scipione was made cardinal. Among the many titles which he held in that period, Scipione was entrusted with care of the art collection and cultural treasures of the pontifical court. With the help of two able architects, Flaminio Ponzio and Giovanni Van Santen (also known as Vasanzio), Cardinal Scipione created the park and built the **Casino Borghese** (Villa Pinciana), today the site of the BORGHESE MUSEUM AND GALLERY.

Galleria Nazionale d'Arte Antica. Raphael's La Fornarina.

One of the most famous streets in the world, Via Veneto is known for its elegance.

Scipione was a passionate collector of art and a bold, attentive patron, he sponsored various artists, including Bernini, Caravaggio, Domenichino, Guido Reni and Rubens, and wanted to build the Casino to serve as a cultural landmark where innumerable works of art would be brought together. The villa was also the diplomatic headquarters of the pontifical court, projecting a full sense of the re-risen magnificence of Ancient Rome and setting the example for a new style: the Roman Baroque. Even the surrounding park was once a permanent exhibit in the open-air of statues, fountains and antique sculptures made for Scipione Borghese, including those used to decorate the welcoming façade of the Casino, with a stairway resembling that of the Cam-

Museo Borghese, Apollo and Dafne *by Bernini*

Pauline Bonaparte, *by Antonio Canova.*

pidoglio, designed by Flaminio Ponzio.

Later, between 1770 and 1800, Marcantonio IV Borghese made notable improvements and enlarged the park, adding the *Giardino del Lago* and building many small buildings. Further additions include *Piazza di Siena*, the *Hippodrome* and the *zoological gardens*. A few years later, his son Camillo, who had married Pauline Bonaparte, sister of Napoleon, was forced to cede 334 pieces of the magnificent collection to the Louvre. In 1902, because of a heavy financial loss, Prince Paolo Borghese had to sell Villa Borghese with all that it now contains to the Italian government; the park was turned over to the City of Rome, the Casino with its artwork to the Italian State.

Reopened to the public in 1997 (visits by reservation) after many years of restoration, the Galleria Borghese and its many art treasures can again be admired and enjoyed.

On the first floor, the portico features antique reliefs and sculpture. Above are two 16th century reliefs made from designs by Michelangelo: *Prometheus Bound* and *Leda and the Swan*. The grandiosity of the salon which follows leaves the visitor breathless for the richness of the decorations, stuccoes, gold and colors which adorn it. The fresco on the vault represents the *Apotheosis of Romulus to Jupiter's Olympus*, by the painter Mariano Rossi (1775-1778). On the wall above is a great equestrian monument representing *Marcus Curtius* in the act of throwing himself into the gorge of the Roman Forum, sacrificing himself for the Roman people. Two colossal statues from the 2nd century AD, a

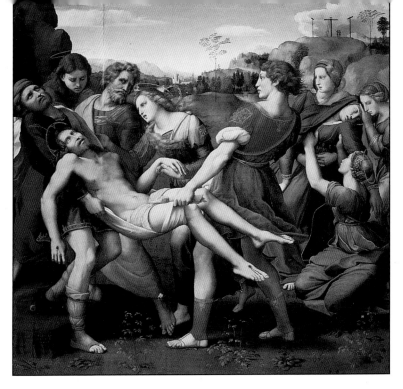

Galleria Borghese. Deposition, *by Raphael.*

Museo Borghese. Rape of Proserpina, *by Bernini.*

Satyr and a *Bacchus*, fill the niches. On the floor is a *mosaic with gladiators* which dates to 320 AD. In the First Room, the visitor's attention is immediately drawn to the neoclassical statue by Canova (1805-1808) of *Pauline Borghese* in the pose of Venus Victrix; on the ceiling the *Judgment of Parides* recalls the subject of the sculpture. The Second Room takes its name from the sculpture at its center, *Bernini's David* (1623), armed with his sling and ready to strike Goliath. For the statue's face and expression, it seems that Bernini used himself in the act of carving the marble as a source of inspiration.

In the center of the Third Room, Bernini's marble group of *Apollo and Daphne* (1622-1625) represents the nymph Daphne transforming herself into a laurel tree to escape from Apollo. The theme of metamorphosis is continued in two paintings by Dosso Dossi, *Circe* and *Apollo and Daphne*. The Fourth Room is called the Room of the Emperors for its many porphyry busts of Roman emperors, although the highlight is Bernini's sculpture of *Pluto and Proserpina* (1621), showing the god of the underworld in the act of kidnapping Proserpina, the daughter of Gea (Earth). The Fifth Room is that of the *Hermaphrodite*, a 1ˢᵗ centu-

Galleria Borghese.
Portrait of a Lady with a
Unicorn, *by Raphael.*

Galleria Borghese.
Boy with a basket of
fruit, *by Caravaggio.*

ry AD sculpture standing in place of a 2nd century AD Hermaphrodite laying on a mattress added by Bernini, which has been in the Louvre since 1807. In the Sixth Room is another magnificent marble group by Bernini, *Aeneas and Anchises* (1618-1620), which represents Aeneas fleeing from Troy, carrying his father Anchises on his shoulders, with his young son Ascanius. The Seventh Room is known as the Egyptian Room. The Eighth Room, called the room of Silenus or the Faun, is dominated by the *Dancing Faun* (2nd century). This room also holds six of the twelve paintings by Caravaggio that once belonged to the collection of Cardinal Scipione.

• The top floor houses the PINACOTHECA, with important 15th-17th century paintings, the original core of which was collected by Cardinal Scipione Borghese. The most important are: in Room IX, *Madonna with Child* by Botticelli, and Raffaello's *Deposition*; in Room X, *Madonna with Child* by Andrea del Sarto, and *Venus and the Angel* by Lucas Cranach the Elder; in Room XIV, six of the twelve Caravaggio paintings collected by Cardinal Borghese, including the *Madonna dei Palafrenieri* and *Boy with a Basket of Fruit*; in Room XV, two self-portraits and a *Portrait of a Youth* by Gianlorenzo Bernini; in Room XIX, Correggio's *Danae* and Titian's *Sacred and Profane Love*.

• After a pleasant stroll along the green avenues of Villa Borghese, we recommend looking out over the terrace of the **PINCIO** gardens, designed by Valadier in 1810. There is a wonderful view from the high terrace: in the distance St. Peter's and the Vatican dominated

by the Dome of Michelangelo, the largest one ever built, in the most brilliant sky. People come here to admire the famous Roman sunsets.

◆ *Viale delle Belle Arti* crosses Villa Borghese, and down on the right is the **Galleria Nazionale d'Arte Moderna**, established in 1883 and later expanded in order to document Italian art of the 19th and 20th centuries, from the Neo-Classicism of Antonio Canova to the more recent trends, like informal art, Pop Art, conceptual and kinetic art.

◆ The road continues to the MUSEOETRUSCO DI VILLA GIULIA, which since 1889 has been home to a collection of Etruscan artifacts from Lazio, Tuscany and Umbria. The villa was built for Pope Julius III by Vignola in 1553, and is a splendid example of a Renaissance villa built as a suburban residence. The exhibit area is in the wings built in 1912 marking the boundaries of the two gardens that flank the central nymphaeum. In the garden to the right there is a late 19th century reconstruction of the Etruscan-Italic temple of Alatri, which serves as a useful introduction for understanding the role of the many finds displayed in the halls. Keep in mind that the museum is laid out by region, i.e, the finds are grouped according to the geographical area from which they came. After the entry hall, devoted to Pyrgi, Cerveteri's port, some rooms fea-

Panoramic view from the Pincio.

Apollo of Veio. *Villa Giulia.*

Museo Etrusco di Villa Giulia, the Sarcophagus of the Married Couple.

On the right, the church of the Trinità dei Monti atop the Spanish Steps.

ture materials from Vulci. Then there are finds from Veio, Cerveteri, and, in various rooms after the semicircle, from *Faleri Veteres* (Civita Castellana). These are followed by discoveries from sites south of Rome like Nemi, Lanuvium, Gabii and Satricum. The thirty-three room exhibit contains important relics including funerary items. Room 5 (Pyrgi) has the *Warrior's Tomb* (6th century BC); Room 7 (Veio) features the famous *Apollo of Veio* (6th century BC); Room 9 (Cerveteri) has the *Sarcophagus of the Married Couple* (6th century BC); Rooms 19-22 contain the *Castellani Collection of Greek* ceramics and precious gold work (the latter can be viewed only with permission); in room 26, the *Faliscan Amphora* by the *"painter of the Dawn"* (4th century BC); in Room 33 (Praeneste), the famous *Ficoroni Cista* (4th century BC), named after the collector, a beautiful bronze toiletries box, finely decorated.

Auditorium - Music Park

Opened in 2002, the Auditorium was designed by architect Renzo Piano and is the most significant work of urban development and culture undertaken in Rome since the 1960's. This is the largest artistic complex of its kind in all of Europe. It consists of a large, acoustically perfect concert hall with 2756 seats; a medium-size 1200-seat hall for both concerts and multimedia shows; a real 700-seat musical theater with an orchestra pit holding sixty players. These three halls are arranged as spokes around a 3,000-seat open-air cavea. The restaurant, bar, bookstore and spaces for shops, recreational activities, studios and exhibits are partially covered by an immense hanging garden. In addition, the remains of a large Roman villa from the Republican Era, dating to 500 BC, associated with a permanent exhibit, make this Music Park truly unique. The complex offers a wide variety of services and activities: classical and contemporary musical events, plays, ballet, movie festivals, and musically-oriented exhibits. The cavea is intended for events of particular significance and for jazz, light and ethnic music.

9 - Along Via del Corso

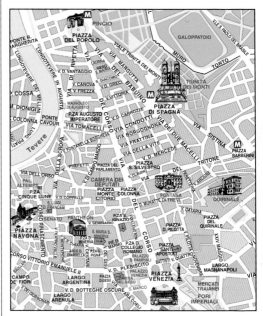

The Temple of Hadrian.

The Trevi Fountain.

♦ The **VIA DEL CORSO** is the principal, most central, and most typical of the old Roman streets. At one end of its narrow but imposingly straight line, nearly a mile long, is the *obelisk* of the Piazza del Popolo; at the other end, the "*Vittoriano*". It is bordered with many papal and princely palaces. The name Corso (race) derived from the special horse races that took place there up to the past century: it replaced the ancient "via Lata". Let us now walk towards the Piazza del Popolo. The first palace we see on the left, the corner palace, is that **of Bonaparte**, where Letitia, mother of Napoleon I, lived and died. Next comes the **Doria-Pamphili palace**, one of the most splendid of papal Rome. The *Doria Gallery* is on the first floor. It is reached by the entrance at the back of the palace, and contains a wealth of 16th and 17th paintings, including the *portrait of Innocent X*, by the Spanish painter Velasquez, three paintings by Caravaggio, including *Rest on the Flight in Egypt*; the

17ᵗʰ century *landscapes* are also interesting. There are also *ancient sculptures* and the *busts of Innocent X* and of *Donna Olimpia*, by Alessandro Algardi.

♦ In the adjacent Piazza di Pietra is the **Temple of Hadrian** (so-called Temple of Neptune). One of its sides, with Corinthian columns, has been beautifully restored. The Stock Exchange now occupies one of its halls.

♦ To the right of the Via del Corso, in the *Via delle Muratte*, is the most sumptuous fountain in Rome. The **FONTANA DI TREVI** is not only celebrated for its excellent water but for the legend that whoever drinks it or throws a coin in the fountain, will assure his return to Rome. It is the façade of a large palace decorated with statues and bas-reliefs on heaps of rocks: the water gushes from every part. The fountain was created by the architect Salvi (1735) under Pope Clement XII, who continued work begun a century previously, in 1641, by Bernini. The reliefs decorating the façade include the one on the right representing the legend about Agrippa's soldiers. It is said that the soldiers of Agrippa, looking for water in the via Collatina in the country, met a maiden who showed them the source of this pure water, which was hence called Virgin Water.

♦ Almost half way down of the Corso is the

Aerial view of Trevi Fountain.

The Column of Marcus Aurelius at Piazza Colonna.

Palazzo Chigi, the offices of the President of the Council of Ministers.

Piazza Colonna, with the **Column of Marcus Aurelius**. After the death of the Emperor-philosopher, the Senate erected a temple and a column in his honour. The column was surmounted by a bronze statue of the Emperor. On the square is the **Chigi Palace**, the Prime Minister's Office. On the opposite side of the Corso is the *Colonna Gallery*.

♦ The **Montecitorio Palace** on the square close by with the same name is the headquarters of the Chamber of Deputies. Of the building built by Bernini between 1653 and 1655, only the slightly convex façade remains. In the early 20th century, the architect Basile adapted the interior and rear parts of the building as the seat of parliament.

♦ To the left, at the corner with Via Fontanella Borghese, we can admire the grand and austere **Palazzo Ruspoli**, built in the 16th century and today an exhibition hall.

♦ Continuing, we come to the *Largo Goldoni*. From here, by the Via Condotti, we reach the **PIAZZA DI SPAGNA**. The first thing that strikes one is the charming, monumental flight of steps (1772) whose sinuous lines harmoniously follow

A striking view of the Spanish steps in piazza di Spagna.

Along Via del Corso

97

the slope of the hill. At its feet is the graceful **Fountain of the "Barcaccia"** by P. Bernini. On the right, in the next square, Piazza Mignanelli, is the column of the Immaculate Conception, a monument erected to commemorate the proclamation of the Dogma (1856). At the top of the Spanish steps is the Church of the **TRINITÀ DEI MONTI**, with its two cupolas (1495), and in front of its facade is an obelisk, which was taken from the Sallustian gardens in 1789. Inside the church, the masterpiece of Daniele da Volterra, the famous fresco of the Descent from the Cross.

Returning to the Via del Corso, we see to our left the baroque church of **St. Charles in the Corso**. At the main altar the Glory of St. Ambrose and St. Charles by Maratta. The heart of St. Charles is kept here in a rich reliquary. Going to the back of the church we admire the outside of the magnificent tribune.

♦ Back on Via del Corso, on the left we find *Piazza Augusto Imperatore* with the **Mausoleum of Augustus**. Built as the tomb of the emperor and his family, over the centuries the monument underwent various transformations: turned into a fortress in the 12th century by the Colonnas, then dismantled and used as a marble quarry, it was even adapt-

Palazzo Montecitorio, where the Chamber of Deputies sits. The Egyptian obelisk of Psammetic II (594-589 BC) stands in the lovely piazza in front of the building

ed as a concert hall (known for its acoustics) until 1936. Farther along, on the Lungotevere along Via Ripetta stands the **Ara Pacis Augustae**, the historic monument erected by Emperor Augustus in 9 BC to celebrate the return to peace throughout the Roman world.

Towards the end of Via del Corso, at number 20, is the **Goethe Museum**, in the house where the great poet lived during his intense stay in Rome. Outstanding are the drawings and sketches that document the artist's multifaceted talent.

The Ara Pacis Augustae has been on display at the monumental complex designed by Richard Meier since 2006.

Piazza del Popolo with the "twin" churches Santa Maria in Montesanto and Santa Maria dei Miracoli.

♦ **Piazza del Popolo** was designed by Valadier at the turn of the century. It is an enormous square, architecturally superb and perfectly symmetrical. In the centre stands the city's second **obelisk**, which was brought to Rome by Augustus, and re-erected here by Fontana under Sixtus V (1589).

According to the legend, in the early middle ages Nero's spirit haunted this place where his ashes had

been deposited in the Domitian family's tomb.
◆ This is why the people destroyed the Mausoleum and built a church there, SANTA MARIA DEL POPOLO, one of the most interesting in Rome. It was probably built in the 11th century, but it was completely reconstructed in the early Renaissance. Among the many works of art to be seen here are: *Adoration of the Child*, by Pinturicchio on the altar of the first chapel on the right; a *Tabernacle* by Andrea Bregno, in the Sacristy; two monuments by Sansovino: to *Cardinal della Rovere*, on the right, and to *Cardinal Sforza*, on the left of the high altar. On the ceiling, the *Coronation of the Virgin* and other frescoes by Pinturicchio; two masterpieces by Caravaggio: *Saul on the road to Damascus*, on one side, the *Crucifixion of St. Peter*, on the other, in a chapel of the transept on the left.

The **Chigi chapel**, the second in the left aisle, was designed by Raphael; it is a real jewel of the Renaissance. On the altar, the *Nativity of the Virgin*, by Sebastiano del Piombo; at the corners, four prophets: *Johan* by Lorenzetto, *Daniel* by Bernim, *Eliah* by Lorenzetto and *Habakkuk* by Bernini. On the sides, the Tombs of the Chigi family.

Piazza del Popolo admired from the terrace of the Pincio gardens.

Santa Maria del Popolo, The Crucifixion of St. Peter *by Caravaggio.*

10 - Campo Marzio and Castel Sant'Angelo

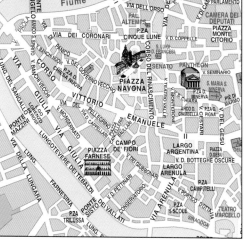

Palazzo Farnese.

♦ On the piazza of the same name stands the **Chiesa del Gesù**, a prototype of the Counterreformation church, built according to the liturgical dictates of the Council of Trent (1545-1563). Built in 1568-1584 to a design by Vignola, its interior features the Baroque **chapel of Saint Ignatius of Loyola**, with its precious niche covered in lapis lazuli and statues of the saint and angels, originally in silver but today in silver stucco.

♦ The **Fountain of the Tortoises**, in little *Piazza Mattei*, is one of the most charming in Rome; its beauty and gracious lines led people to believe that this artistic jewel of the late 16th century had been designed by Raphael. It was actually built by Giacomo della Porta, and the bronzes are by Taddeo Landini (1585).

♦ At *Largo di Torre Argentina* is the **Sacred Area of Largo Argentina**, the most extensive complex from the Republican period that is still visible. The remains of the four temples, which date from the 4th to the 2nd centuries B.C., are not imposing for their size, but interesting for their architectural form and age.

The Fountain of the Tortoises.

The Sacred Area of Largo Argentina, the most extensive complex from the Republican area currently on view. The temple in the foreground dates to the mid-3ʳᵈ century B.C.

♦ SANT'ANDREA DELLA VALLE was designed by Maderno and built between 1591 and 1650. The cupola is the highest in Rome after St. Peter's, and also one of the most beautiful. The imposing facade, in travertine, is the work of Carlo Rainaldi.

The interior is in the form of a Latin cross, with an spacious nave and large side chapels; the apse, the vault and the cupola combine to give an impression of splendor and solemnity. The Ginnetti-Lancellotti chapel (first on the right) is by Carlo Fontana. The solemn and austere Strozzi (second) is a superb work by Giacomo della Porta, based on designs by Michelangelo.

On the altar, the **Pietà** between **Leah** and **Rachael**, is a perfect reproduction in bronze of the noted works by Michelangelo. The four

The statue of Giordano Bruno in the middle of Campo de' Fiori.

A typical corner of Campo de' Fiori

Santa Maria sopra Minerva. Statue of Christ Carrying the Cross, *sculpted by Michelangelo.*

On the right the "Pulcin della Minerva" consisting of an Egyptian obelisk of the VI century BC and a little elephant designed by Bernini.

The façade of the Pantheon.

tombs in black marble rest members of the Strozzi family.

♦ **Campo de' Fiori** was for a long time the site of public executions. On February 17th, 1600, the heretic philosopher *Giordano Bruno* was burned here; the monument is the work of Ferrari (1887). The lively market makes this piazza a typical part of Old Rome.

♦ The superb **Palazzo Farnese** on the piazza of the same name, was begun during the papacy of Paul III by Antonio da Sangallo the Younger (1514), continued by Michelangelo (1546), who added the marvelous cornices, the central window and part of the courtyard, and then completed in 1589 by Giacomo della Porta. This majestic national monument was already the seat of the French embassy when it was ceded to France in 1908.

♦ The beautiful, large 13th century church of SANTA MARIA SOPRA MINERVA (1280-1290) was designed by the same Domenican friars who built Santa Maria Novella in Florence. With its moderately acute arches supported by high cross-shaped pilasters which divide the naves, this church is a rare example of Gothic architecture in Rome. The name "sopra Minerva" (above Minerva) refers to an ancient temple to Minerva Calcidica, over which the church was built. Under the high altar rests the **body of St. Catherine of Siena** (1347-1380) in a marble sarcophagus. The saint dedicated a great part of her energy to bringing the papacy back from Avignon. After Pope Gregory XI returned the papacy to Rome, St. Catherine retired to the convent adjacent to the church, where she lived her last days. Her letters to kings, popes and others had a great political importance, a spiritual tone, and a high literary value.

To the left of the altar is the famous **statue of Christ Carrying the Cross**, sculpted by Michelangelo between 1514 and 1521. In the left transept is the stone monument of **Brother Giovanni from Fiesole** (1387-1455), one of the great painters of the 15th century in Italy, better known as Beato Angelico. In the choir are the mon-

umental tombs of the two Medici popes of the Renaissance, Leo X (1513-21) and Clement VII (1523-34) by Antonio da Sangallo the Younger.

The **Egyptian Obelisk of Minerva** once stood in front of the ancient Temple of Isis, and was erected in the piazza of the same name by Pope Alexander VII in 1667. Bernini had it mounted on the back of an elephant that was sculpted by Ferrata, one of his best assistants.

♦ The **PANTHEON** - the glory of Rome - is the city's only architecturally intact monument from classical times. Because of the inscription on the cornice of the portico, "*M. Agrippa L.F. Cos. tertium fecit*", for a long time it was believed that the Pantheon, as it stands today, had been built by Agrippa in 27 B.C. and dedicated to the gods of the Julian family; his temple was actually destroyed by a fire in 80 A.D., and completely redesigned by Hadrian. Other restoration was

The Pantheon. In the middle of Piazza della Rotonda the wonderful fountain designed by Giacomo della Porta surmounted by the little obelisk of Ramsses II.

The Pantheon reconstructed in reduced scale.

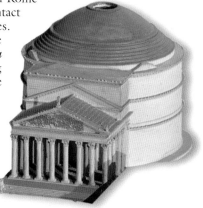

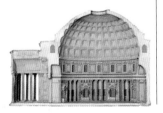

The inside of the Pantheon measures 43,4 meters in width and height. Some of Italy's most famous kings and artists are buried here.

Section of the Pantheon.

done under Septimius Severus and by Caracalla in the 3rd century.

On March 16, 609 A.D., Pope Boniface IV, with the permission of the Emperor Phocas, changed the pagan temple into a Christian church, bringing the bones of many Christians from the catacombs and dedicating it to "St. Mary of the Martyrs," thus ensuring the preservation of the building to this day.

In 1929 the church, as a result of the Lateran Treaty, assumed the title of the Basilica Palatina, or more properly, the national church of all Italians.

The **portico** has 16 monolithic granite columns. In the tympanum there was once a bronze relief which depicted the Battle of the Gods and the Giants. The ceiling of the portico was covered in bronze, but the precious material, almost 450,000 pounds, was taken down by Pope Urban VIII (1623-1644), and used by Bernini for the baldacchino (canopy) in St. Peter's and other works. In the niches were once statues of Augustus and Agrippa. The **bronze doors** are original.

The **interior** measures 43.4 meters in width and height. Light and air enters through the opening at the top (an oculus, almost 9 meters across, which features some of the original bronze), through which the sky seems to descend to the temple and in turn prayers freely rise to the heavens. The Pantheon's simple regularity, the beauty of its elements, and its splendid materials combine to give the interior a sublime solemnity.

The **cupola** is in reality a cap whose thickness diminishes as it rises. Around the perimeter are seven niches: in the niche opposite the entrance was once a statue to Mars Ultor, who had punished the murderers of Caesar; in the others, statues of Mars and Romulus, Aeneas, Julius Ascanius and of Julius Caesar; other gods and heroes were in the intermediate spaces. The splendid giallo antico marble columns testify to the temple's original magnificence.

In the first chapel on the left rest the bones of **Perin del Vaga** (1500-47), considered, along with Giulio Romano, as the best of Raphael's

The building attached to the rear of the Pantheon is all that remains of the Basilica of Neptune. This was part of a vast monumental complex done by Agrippa, the main collaborator of Augustus. Like the Pantheon, the Basilica of Neptune was heavily restored by Hadrian, to whose style the apse can be traced, topped by a marble architrave decorated with dolphins and shells.

San Luigi dei Francesi. The Calling of Saint Matthew, *by Caravaggio.*

assistants. Nearby is the **tomb** of the great painter and architect **Baldassare Peruzzi** (1481-1536). In the second chapel are the **tombs of King Umberto I di Savoia** (1844-1900) and **Queen Margherita** (1851-1926). Between the second and third chapel is a tomb containing the remains of **Raphael** (1483-1520), the most popular among all the painters in the world, whose epigraph says "Here lies Raphael. Living, great Nature feared he might outvie her works, and dying, fears she herself may die."

The **statue of the Madonna** is the work of his assistant, Lorenzetto. Nearby is the **tomb of Maria Bibbiena**, Raphael's fiancée, who died three months before he. Above is the tombstone by **Annibale Caracci** (1560-1609).

In the third chapel is the cenotaph of **Cardinal Consalvi** (1755-1824), an exquisite work by Thorwaldsen. In the same chapel, the **tomb of Vittorio Emanuele II di Savoia**, the first king of Italy (1820-1878). On the altar of the seventh chapel is a 15th century fresco of the **Annunciation** by Melozzo da Forli'.

Piazza Navona. The Fountain of the Rivers built in 1651 by Bernini. The Egyptian-style obelisk is a Roman copy.

The fountain of the Calderari.

◆ **PIAZZA NAVONA**, or *Circus Agonale*, traces the shape of the Stadium of Domitian, which once occupied this site and held 30,000 spectators. Interesting remains of the ancient structure visible north of the piazza. Three magnificent fountains decorate the piazza: In the center - "an Aesop's fable fashioned in marble" - is the **Fountain of the Four Rivers** by Bernini, who designed it as a base for the Egyptian obelisk which was brought here from the Circus of Maxentius. Four figures seated on

Piazza Navona. Exciting naval battles were once staged in the Stadium of Domitian, now Piazza Navona.

Palazzo Altemps

The palace, begun before 1477 by Girolamo Riario, was finished by Cardinal Marco Sittico Altemps and his heirs around 1570. In the sixteenth century, Cardinal Altemps gathered a large collection of antique sculpture and an extremely rich library, which were subsequently broken up. The palace, restored by the Superintendent of Archaeology of Rome, is today home to the **Ludovisi Boncompagni Collection**, the **Egyptian Collection** of the Museo Nazionale Romano, the **Mattei Collection**, some pieces from other collections, and just sixteen sculptures that remain from the Altemps collection. The Ludovisi Boncompagni Collection was begun by Cardinal Ludovico Ludovisi between 1621 and 1623 in a villa on the Quirinal Hill, and was enriched over the years, especially by the new owner of the Villa Gregorio Boncompagni; by the 19th century it contained 339 sculptures. Many works were brought together through state acquisitions in 1901.

There are many works of great interest on the ground floor of the palazzo. The courtyard is without doubt the most remarkable, having been worked on by Antonio Sangallo the Elder, Baldassarre Peruzzi and Martino Longhi. Built at the same time as the courtyard, the southern portico is decorated with family crests of the Orsini and Altemps. Like the northern portico, it holds sculptures from the Mattei collection of the Villa Celimontana. The atrium is named after *Antonino Pius* for the nude statue of an emperor which it hosts. Also on the first floor are ten display rooms rich with statues, sarcophagi, portraits, herms and ornamental vases. Among them are the beautiful statues of *Apollo Citaredo*, the *Athena* (with head and limbs restored by Algardi), and the *Athena Parthenos* from the Ludovisi Collection. Also notable is the *colossal group of Dionysius*, the *Satyr and the panther*, a Roman copy of a Greek original. A monumental stairway leads to the first floor, which contains the Southern Loggia and the Painted Loggia; many display rooms; the private rooms of the Cardinal, with several busts; and those of the Duchessa Isabella Lante Altemps, with the *Bathing Aphrodite* by Diodalsas, *Eros and Psyche*, a composition of ancient works created by Algardi.

In the Room of the Fireplace is *Galata Killing himsel, with his wife*, to which belonged the *Dying Galata* which hangs today in the Capitoline Museums.

Above, the Apollo Citaredo.

Below, the Galatian suicide with his wife.

the rocks represent the Nile, Ganges, Danube and the Rio de la Plata.

The fountain on the south side of the piazza, called the **Fountain of the Moor**, was designed by Giacomo della Porta between 1571 and 1576, but his statues of tritons and masks were later moved to the Giardino del Lago in the Villa Borghese; the statues on the fountain are 19th century copies. The fountain

takes its name from the statue of the Moor, which Bernini added in the 17th century. At the north end of the piazza is the **Fountain of the Calderari** (Coppersmiths), so-called because of the many workshops in the area. This fountain also lost some of its original statues and its sculptural decoration was only completed in the 19th century.

◆ The church of **Sant'Agnese in Agone** is a magnificent example of the Baroque style by G. Rainaldi and Borromini. It was built on the site, where according to tradition, the virgin was stripped naked before being martyred, and miraculously hair grew to cover her body. Underneath the church are remains of a primitive church and the Stadium of Domitian.

◆ Nearby is the majestic **Ponte Sant'Angelo** (once called Ponte Elio), adorned by a double row of *angels* sculpted by followers of Bernini. The bridge was built by Emperor Hadrian (130 A.D.) together with the mausoleum which is now the **CASTEL SANT'ANGELO** (Castle St. Angel). That which seems to be

Piazza Navona.
The fountain of the Moor.

Palazzo Altemps.
The Ludovisi Throne.

an impregnable fortress was created by the Emperor Hadrian as his tomb. The Mole of Hadrian, or "*Hadrianeum*", was begun in 123 A.D. and held the remains of the Imperial family until Caracalla (217 A.D.) From what remains it is impossible to understand its original scale; a great deal of imagination is required to reconstruct the majestic structure. Procopius, the 6th century Byzantine historian,

left a description of how the mausoleum appeared in his day: it had a square base, above which rose a great tower decorated by Doric columns, statues and spaces for the epitaphs of the buried. On the top was a colossal bronze group which represented Hadrian on a chariot drawn by four horses; all the walls, of enormous thickness, were covered in Parian marble. It was, together with the Colosseum, the most splendid example of Roman architecture.

The story of the Mausoleum of Hadrian closely follows that of the city of Rome: the struggles and treachery of the Middle Ages, the splendor of the Papal Court and the Renaissance, the horrors of the Sack of Rome of 1527, the intense bombardment during many sieges, and the fireworks of many celebrations. Under Aurelian (275 A.D.), or more probably under Honorius (403 A.D.), it was strongly fortified and incorporated into the city walls. It included 6 towers, 164 merlons, 14 platforms for artillery and 18 loopholes, and defended the western bank of the

Above, Castel Sant'Angelo as it appears today; below, graphic reconstruction of Hadrian's Mausoleum. It was on the mausoleum's ruins that today's fortress was built.

Tiber. This strategic function was demonstrated during the first invasion of the barbarians, led by Alaric in 410.

The transformation into a castle probably occurred in the 10th century, when it became the possession of Alberic and his mother, Marozia, powerful figures in Rome at the time. It then passed to the Crescenzi family and in 1277 was occupied by Pope Nicholas III, who joined it to the Vatican by the famous **passetto** (passageway), a corridor which runs atop the

wall that encircles the Vatican. This long fortified passageway allowed the pope to safely walk
from the Vatican to the Castle. From that time
on the Castle remained under control of the
popes, who used it as a fortress and official
palace, but also as a prison and place of torture.

The name Castel Sant'Angelo (Castle St.
Angel) dates to the 12th century, but is rooted in
a much older legend. During a solemn procession in 590 led by St. Gregory the Great to
implore the Virgin to put an end to a plague
which was devastating the city, an angel appeared
in the sky and landed above the mausoleum,
sheathing his sword as a sign of grace granted. A
chapel was then built in honor of the angel, followed by a statue which recalled the miracle;
eventually the whole building was renamed.

The Castle is steeped in memories of blood-
shed and crime, and famous prisoners were
held there. In 1527 the city was occupied by
invaders led by Carlo V, who besieged in the
fortress. From the "passetto", Pope Clement
VII witnessed the horrible abuses, theft and
sacrilege.

Castel Sant'Angelo can be divided in five
floors: First floor (or groundfloor), at which

Ponte and Castel Sant'Angelo.

Castel Sant'Angelo's name dates back to the 12th century but has its origins in a much older legend. During a solemn procession in 590 by Pope Gregory the Great to beseech the Virgin to put an end to the plague that was devastating the city, an angel appeared in the sky and came to rest atop the Mausoleum, sheathing his sword as a sign that the plea was being answered. A chapel was then built in honor of the Angel, and later a statue was added to evoke the miracle. The building's name was then changed to recall the event.

Castel Sant'Angelo in an 18ᵗʰ century painting.

Castel Sant'Angelo by night.

begins the famous 125 meter long helicoidal ramp, a splendid Roman construction. (After the ramp, continue up to the left along the **ramp of Pope Alexander VI** which leads directly to the third floor and the Courtyard of the Angel). Second Floor (or floor of the prisons). It is reached from the Courtyard of Pope Alexander VI on the third floor. Here famous prisoners were once held, such as Arnaldo da Brescia and Benvenuto Cellini, while even more horrid cells - called historic prisons - were reserved for less illustrious guests

Third Floor (or Military Floor). Here there are two great courtyards: the **Courtyard of the Angel**, with the **Marble Angel** by Raffaello da Montelupo in the middle, which stood atop the castle until 1752, and the **Courtyard of Pope Alexander VI** with a lovely 16ᵗʰ century **marble well**. A narrow stairway leads up to the interesting small **Bathroom of Pope Clement VII**, with frescoes by Giulio Romano.

Fourth Floor (or papal floor) with the **Loggia of Pope Julius II**, by Sangallo, at the front of the Castle and the papal apartment composed of magnificent rooms frescoed by Giulio Romano, Perin del Vaga and other followers of Raphael.

The **Treasure Room** or secret archive room, still furnished with wardrobes from the time of Pope Paul III which contained private documents. This room and the one above it formed the burial chamber of Hadrian. The room of the Cagliostra was the prison of the celebrated alchemist of the 18th century.

The **Pauline Room**, or Council Room, decorated by Perin del Vaga (1545) has the richest decorations; on the vault are the frescoes of the deeds of Alexander the Great. On the walls, trompe-l'oeil columns separate scenes dedicated to Alexander, Hadrian and the Archangel Michael. Fifth Floor (or last floor). The great terrace offers a magnificent panorama of the city. Above towers the **Bronze Archangel** by Verschaffelt (1753, recently restored).

Aerial view of St. Peter's Square and Via della Conciliazione. In the background, Castel Sant'Angelo. Parallel to Via della Conciliazione, on the left, the "passetto" is visible: an escape route, elevated and fortified, linking the Vatican to Castel Sant'Angelo. During a siege, the passetto allowed popes and clergy to withdraw quickly and safely from the Vatican palaces to the more secure refuge of Castel Sant'Angelo.

*The Tiara and the Keys,
symbols of pontifical
authority.*

*St. Peter's Basilica
illuminated.*

11 - The Vatican

The **VATICAN** has been the residence of the popes only since 1377, six centuries interrupted by long stays at the Quirinal Palace. Before the pontifical court was transferred to Avignon (1309-1377), the headquarters of the pope had been at the Lateran.

Since then, there has not been a pope who has failed to contribute to the grandeur and dignity of the Vatican, to make this holy hill an increasingly worthy seat for the Supreme Head of the Catholic Church. An uninterrupted succession of 265 men have sat on St. Peter's throne, many of whom were martyrs and saints. The Vatican has been an independent state (called the **Vatican City**) since February 11, 1929, when the *Lateran Treaty* definitively resolved the "Roman Issue" between the Church and the Italian State.

In Roman times, the Vatican was the site of the great Circus of Nero, where under Nero, St. Peter was crucified (circa 64 - 67 A.D.). His body was buried nearby; more than 250 years later, Constantine built a magnificent basilica on the spot, which was destined to become one of the marvels of the world. During the 73 years that the papacy was in Avignon, the already old basilica was so neglected that restoration was impossible. Pope Nicolas V (1447-1455) decided to rebuild it, and gave the project to Rossellino, but after the pope's death, all work was suspended. It was Pope Julius II (1503-1513) who began the construction of a new basilica, entrusting Bramante with the design

of the great architectural project, which took 176 years to complete. Until Michelangelo, then almost seventy years old, began to build the dome, there had been a succession of various architects, among them Raphael and Antonio da Sangallo the Younger, and different plans. After Michelangelo's death, the work went on according to his designs, which called for Bramante's original Greek cross plan, but under the papacy of Paul V (1605-1621), Maderno decisively adopted a Latin cross design for the new basilica.

The greatest church in Christendom, **ST. PETER'S BASILICA**, rises on the grandiose **St. Peter's Square**. Michelangelo's mighty silver-blue dome dominates the scene, blending into the sky above, conveying a sense of the absolute and infinite, which touches the soul of all who gaze upon it. The construction of the dome proceeded through problems and obstacles of every kind. Michelangelo was already quite old when he began the project in 1546, and when he died in 1564 only the drum had been completed. The rest of the work was finished between 1588 and 1589 by Giacomo della Porta and Domenico Fontana.

The **Colonnade** is Bernini's most beautiful work, and forms the solemn entrance to St. Peter's and the Vatican. The two great open semicircular wings seem as if they were the outstretched arms of the church, receiving all of mankind in one universal embrace. If some of Bernini's other works appear to be extravagant, this colonnade shows the height of his genius. He also designed the 140 *statues of saints* which decorate the colonnade,

The façade of St. Peter's, designed by Maderno. Note the warm shades of the marble, rediscovered after the major restoration work done for the Jubilee 2000.

The polychrome figure of the Holy Spirit in the form of a dove.

MAP OF ST. PETER

1) Atrium.
2) Mosaic of the Navicella.
3) Central Door.
4) Door by Manzù.
5) Holy Door.
6) Nave.
7) Statue of St. Peter.
8) Papal Altar.
9) Statue of St. Longino.
10) Canopy.
11) Confession.
12) Chapel of the Pietà.
13) Chapel of St. Sebastian with the Tomb of Blessed John Paul II.
14) Chapel of the Blessed Sacrament.
15) Gregorian Chapel.
16) Right Transept.
17) St. Peter's Trone.
18) Chapel of the Column.
19) Left Transept.
20) Clementine Chapel.
21) Chapel of the Choir.
22) Chapel of the Presentation of the Virgin.
23) Baptistery.
24) The Treasury.

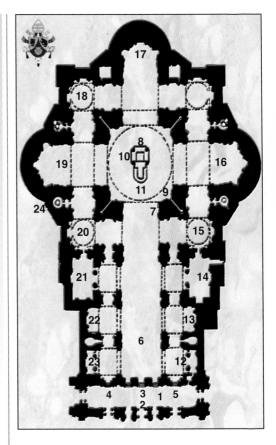

A fresco of the old Constantinian Basilica.

which were sculpted with the help of his pupils. Pope Sixtus V (1585-1590) chose Domenico Fontana to oversee the erection of the **Obelisk** in the middle of the piazza, a considerable task which aroused wonder and great enthusiasm in the people. The obelisk measures more than 25 meters in height and was brought from the nearby ruins of the Circus of Nero. The **two fountains**, the one on the right designed by Maderno (1613) and the one on the left by Carlo Fontana (1675), harmonize beautifully with the vast square. The Borghese Pope Paul V commissioned Maderno (1607-1614) to construct the broad **façade** of the church, and had his name and title written in very large letters across the entablature. The **Loggia of the Benediction**, above the central entrance, is used to proclaim the election of a new pope, and it is from here that he delivers his first blessing, "Urbi et Orbi" (to the city and the world).

Inside the **portico**, above the principal entrance, is the famous *mosaic of the Navicella* (little boat), designed for the old basilica by Giotto during the first Holy Year (1300), which has undergone considerable restoration. Five doors open onto the portico, corresponding to the five aisles in the basilica. The first door on the left is the *Door of Death* by Manzu', which shows the death of Jesus and that of the Madonna, the death of Pope John XXIII and death in space (1952-1964).

The *Bronze Door* in the center came from the old basilica; it was designed by Filarete as an imitation of the doors by Ghiberti in Florence.

The **Holy Door** on the far right is only opened every twenty-five years, at the beginning of the Holy Year. On Christmas Eve, the Pope, according to a special ritual, makes a solemn procession to this door, and after a triple genuflection and three strokes of a hammer, the wall is removed and the Pope is the first to cross the threshold and enter the basilica. At the end of the Holy Year the door is re-closed with a solemn ceremony. The modern reliefs which decorate the door are the work of Vico Consorti. Another two contemporary doors complete the portico: the *Door of Good and Evil* by Minguzzi and the *Door of the Sacraments* by Crocetti.

Entering the church, one is struck by the enormity of the basilica. The numbers speak eloquently: the length of the interior of the

St. Peter's dome seen from the Tiber.

Aerial view of St. Peter's Square and Basilica.

St. Peter's Square is the largest in Rome (314 meters long by 240 meters wide). A beautiful Egyptian obelisk, 25 meters high, stands at its center.

basilica, as shown in an inscription in the pavement near the bronze door, is 186.36 meters (the external length, including the portico, is 211.5 meters). Other signs in the floor indicate the lengths of the major churches in the world; the vault is 44 meters high; the dome, measured from the inside, measures 119 meters, with the lantern adding another 17 meters; the perimeter of one of the four piers which support the dome measures 71 meters.

At the end of the immense central nave rises the bronze **baldacchino** (canopy) which covers the high altar - its 29 meters makes it 4 meters taller than the obelisk on the piazza. One of the most significant objects that was transferred from the old basilica is the *porphyry disk* at the beginning of the nave, upon which Charlemagne knelt on Christmas Day 800 to be consecrated Holy Roman Emperor by Pope Leo III.

Near the transept is the celebrated 13th century **bronze statue of St. Peter**, set against one of the enormous pilasters which supports Michelangelo's dome. In the niches at the bases of the pilasters are four statues: **San Longino** by Bernini, the **Empress St. Helena** by Andrea Bolgi, **St. Veronica** by Francesco Mochi, and

The Tomb of St. Peter.

St. **Andrea** by Francois Du-
quesnoy. The high altar, under
the cupola, rises above the **Tomb
of St. Peter**, which was definitively
identified after excavations in the
1950's. In front of the tomb,
ninety-nine lamps burn day and
night; opposite is the **crypt**,
designed by Maderno, rich
with inlaid marble. Above the
altar rises Bernini's fantastic
baldacchino (1633), supported by four spiral columns,
made from bronze taken from
the Pantheon. But the glorification of
the tomb of the humble fisherman from the Galilee
is the majestic **dome** that soars toward the heavens.

Michelangelo's Pietà.

Returning toward the entrance, in the first
chapel of the right nave is Michelangelo's
Pietà, sculpted between 1498 and 1499. The
deep pathos that animates the group, in which
the eternally young Mother and the dead Son
leaning down in her arms make an indissoluble
whole, reminds us that this subjet was strongly
felt by Michelangelo.

On the aisle, walking toward the transept,
we find one across from the other the first two
important funeral monuments: leaning on
against the first pillar that appears at the main
aisle arises the *Monument dedicated to
Christine of Sweden*, one of the most famous
Queens of history. Opposite it is placed the
Monument dedicated to Pope Leo XII (1823-

The statue of St. Peter,
attributed to A. di Cambio.

The central nave of St. Peter's Basilica.

The Holy water stoup *is supported by gigantic cherubs (1725).*

1829), beneath which there is the entrance to the *Chapel of the Relics*, of elliptical shape open at the inside of the first lateral pillar of the aisle. The Chapel is also called of the *Crucifix* for the valuable medieval wooden masterpiece, representing *Jesus on the Cross* attributed to the Roman artist of the thirteenth century, Pietro Cavallini. The next *Chapel of Saint Sebastian* is so called for the mosaic with which it is decorated reproducing the *Martyrdom of Saint Sebastian*, taken from an altarpiece by Domenichino. The chapel contains the **Tomb of Blessed John Paul II**, who was entombed here after his beatification ceremony on 1 May 2011 when his body was moved from the Vatican Grottoes where it was laid to rest in 2005.

On the aisle, between this chapel and the next one, we admire two more funeral monuments that remind us, one in front of the other, of a Pontiff and a famous woman of history. It is the Sepolchrus of the 18th century belonging to *Innocent XII* in front of which is placed the *Monument to Countess*

Matilde of Canossa. The monument was a project of Bernini, while the statue of the Countess was sculptured by his scholar Andrea Bolgi.

A few steps away, on the right, there is the vast *Chapel of the Blessed Sacrament* in which the Holy Species are kept in a somptuous golden bronze *tabernacle* which is by Gianlorenzo Bernini. And here we are at last at the or *Gregorian Chapel* or *Chapel of Madonna del Soccorso* that took its first name from Pope Gregory XIII; in fact, he entrusted the construction of the Chapel to Giacomo della Porta the year of the Reform. The other name is given by the small painting of the 12th Century from the Constantine Basilica representing the *Madonna del Soccorso*.

Continuing along on the right we find, opposite to another important artistic masterpiece, the *Monument in memory of Clement XIII* by Canova, in which the rather cold elegance sober of the great neo-classic sculptor shows the spirit of his age.

In the next passage there are placed the *Monument to Clement X* in which we notice above all the relief representing the Opening of the Holy Door, in occasion of the Jubilee Year 1675, and the altar with the altar-piece in mosaic representing *Saint Peter reviving Tabita*. From here we overlook the stately *apse* the centre of which consists of the **throne**, that bears the characteristic signs of the

The Chair of St. Peter, a theatrical work by Bernini in gilded bronze.

St. Peter's Basilica. Altar of the Falsehood.

On the right. St. Peter's Basilica. The statue of Innocent VIII by Pollaiolo.

St. Peter's Basilica. Altar of the Sacred Heart.

original art of Gianlorenzo Bernini. The throne is supported by gigantic figures of two Fathers of the Latin Church, Saint Agostino and Saint Ambrogio, and two figures of the Greek Church, Saint Atanasio and Saint Giovanni Crisostomo. The tiara and the keys, symbols of papal authority, supported by small angels, surmont the Throne itself, concentrating the value symbolically. Above all, at last, there is the round window full of light with the polychrome figure of the dove representing *Holy Ghost* surrounded by a phantasmagoric nimbus of glorifying angels.

On the right side we can see the *Monument in memory of Urban VIII* a work of Bernini himself, although realized more than twenty years before the realization of the Chair, shows a perfect equilibrium between sculpture and architecture, that was one of the most significant merits of the artist.

We arrive at the *Chapel of the Column*. Its name comes from a column derived from the Constantine Old Basilica, on which an adored image of the *Blessed Virgin* is painted, placed on an Altar.

The Chapel features out the singular marble altar-piece in relief by Alessandro Algardi, representing the *encounter between Saint Leo Magnus and Attila*. It is one of the main monuments of the Christian Middle Ages.

On the *left aisle*, there is the grand *Clementine Chapel* or *Chapel of Saint Gregory Magnus*. Its first denomination derives from Pope Clement VIII, under whom it was built by Giacomo della Porta. The main altar, in which the *remains of Saint Gregory Magnus* are venerated, is surmounted by the altar piece in mosaic representing the *Miracle of the cloth* undertaken by the Holy Pontiff himself. Lying on the left wall of the Chapel there is the *Pius VII Monument* (1820-1823), the work of the Danish sculptor Bertel Thorvaldsen, Roman by adoption.

We now admire the *Chapel of the Chorus* that together with that of the Blessed Sacrament, in front of which it is placed on the right aisle, is the widest of the Basilica.

In the passage on the aisle, two monuments built in two distant stages: on the right there is in fact one of the few works of our century that are placed in Saint Peter's Basilica, the *Monument in memory of Pius X* (1903-1914); opposite, an artistic jewel of the Basilica the *Monument in memory of Innocent VIII* (1484-92) by Pollaiolo, formerly standing in the old Basilica.

The *Chapel of the Presentation* named for the altar-piece on the main altar, with the *Presentation*

St. Peter's Basilica.
The superb baldaquin by Bernini during a religious celebration.

of the Blessed Virgin at the Templum, taken from the painting of the 17th century by Giovanni Romanelli. The next passage in the aisle shows us the *Monument to Maria Clementina Sobieski* (1702-1735) of typical 18th century elegance, work of Pietro Bracci. Opposite there is the marvellous *funeral stele of the late Stuarts*, one of the masterpieces of Canova

Our last stop inside the Basilica is at the *Chapel of the Baptistery*, at the centre of which there is the *Baptismal Font* of red porphiry characteristic of the classic age, completed in the 18th century by Carlo Fontana with a new bronze tipically rococò composition.

The interior of the Michelangelo's dome decorated by Cavalier d'Arpino.

THE SACRED GROTTOES

The area below the ground level of the current basilica approximately corresponds to the level of the ancient construction of Constantine and it contains important sites of interest. The entrance to the Vatican Grottoes is found outside the Basilica, next to the entrance to the Cupola on the right side of the portico. Here a small ramp of stairs leads to the **Old Grottoes** which extend beneath the central nave of the upper basilica built by Antonio da Sangallo as an air space to protect the floor of the newer construction from humidity.

In the suggestive semi-darkness between the three naves with flattened arches, marked by a succes-

The majestic dome of St. Peter's, by Michelangelo.

Mosaic from the Constantinian Basilica. Detail of St. Peter preaching to the Romans.

sion of two lines of powerful columns there are around twenty funeral monuments of popes including the tomb of Paul VI and the tomb of John Paul I, an emperor, a king, two queens, numerous cardinals and bishops as well as important art works and remembrances of the construction of Constantine.

Leaving this area we find the true "Sancta Sanctorum" of the Basilica: here we find the **Tomb of St. Peter**, the spiritual centre of the Vatican Grottoes, which is conserved in the so-called **New Grottoes**: in reality this is the oldest part, but it was later restored giving rise to the name. Here, at the end of the fourth century, Pope Gregory the Great placed a stone altar above the monument in the necropolis below where the early Christians venerated the sepulchre of St. Peter (see the inset on pg. 127). Four oratories and some chapels open off of the hallway and the tomb of Pope Pius XII is located in one of them.

Treasury of St. Peter's. The tomb of Sixtus IV by Pollaiolo.

A portrait of St. Peter, Apostol of Christ and the Church's first Pontiff.

THE TREASURY

In the Basilica once again, going up the left aisle to the Monument to Pius VIII, under which is the entrance to the **Sacristy**, one reaches the **Museum of Historical Art of St. Peter's, or the Treasury**. Right from the age of Costantine (4th century) the Basilica of St. Peter received outstanding donations many of which came through the Emperor himself.

The generosity of the donators was such that in

The Vatican Hill and the ancient Constantinian basilica

In Roman times, a circus extended on the sides of the Vatican Hill in the area which corresponds to what is now the left side of St. Peter's Square. It was built by the Emperor Caligula, and at its center stood the obelisk which now stands at the center of the square.

In 67 AD, the Apostle Peter was crucified and was then buried in an anonymous grave in the adjacent necropolis, an event which would mark this spot for eternity. After Nero was killed, the *Circus of Caligula* (or *Circus of Nero*) was abandoned, while the *Vatican Necropolis* became a site holy to the Christian cult. Two hundred fifty years later, the Emperor Constantine, who made Christianity the state religion, had a grandiose basilica built at the foot of the Vatican Hill, in a way so that its apse contained the tomb which the Christians had always considered the tomb of St. Peter. In order to do so, the Emperor had to cut away a part of the Vatican Hill, and with the profanation of the cemetery, created an esplanade that allowed for the excavation of the solid foundation. The church was built in the style of a Roman pagan basilica, although it included important architectural innovations which were adopted and further developed for other Christian religious sites. The grandiosity of the old St. Peter's Basilica was established through five naves intersected by a transept, an important innovation. The various columns were therefore made of different materials, and the marble pavement had pagan inscriptions and reliefs. The façade was decorated with rich mosaics and was preceded by a large atrium. In the background, at the center of the apse, the *tomb of St. Peter* serves as the focal point of the basilica, drawing the attention of the faithful.

Whether the tomb contained the actual remains of the Saint was debated for centuries, and remained more an act of faith than

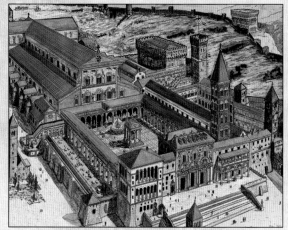

Drawing of the old St. Peter's Basilica, built by the Emperor Constantine.

certainty. But in 1968, Pope Paul VI announced to the world that *"the reliquaries of St. Peter have been identified in a manner which we can consider convincing."* Such a declaration led to long studies, which subsequently provided significant confirmation. The archeologists had concentrated their attention on a tomb toward which all the other tombs of the Vatican Necropolis converged, and on two walls in particular. The first, erected around 160 AD in brick and covered with red plaster, has an inscription *"Petr ... en..."*. The second, which dates to the 3rd century AD and built perpendicular to the first. It was covered with grafitti of the names of the faithful who gathered in prayer in the presence of this venerated tomb, as well as invocations of Christ (of the word in grafitti, which was called *"Muro G"*). Across a cavity from this wall, it is possible to reach human remains exhumed and re-interred here during the construction of the Constantinan Basilica.

Philological studies showed that the inscription *"Petr... en..."* meant, in ancient greek, that "Peter is here.", while scientific analysis supported the hypothesis that the bones found here were those of the Apostle Peter. The coincidence of these two important discoveries, along with other elements, allowed for acceptance of the historical announcement of Pope Paul VI.

the following centuries, the Treasury was assiduously replenished in spite of the frequency with which it was disastrously plundered, especially on the occasion of the various Jubilees which have taken place since 1300.

Room I - There are a red cope with tiara decorated with stones (18th century) destined to cover the venerated Saint Peter's statue of bronze; the so-called *Chalice Stuart*, itself belonging to the 18th century, in gold and silver with 130 mounted brilliants.

Room II - There is the *Dalmatix*, erroneously called *of Charlemagne*.

Room III is dominated by the bronze *monument to Sixtus IV* (1471-84), a masterpiece by Antonio del Pollaiolo.

In Room V - There is a collection of precious chalices and reliquaries.

In Room VI, a vast *collection of candelabra* is exhibited.

Room IX contains the *sarcophagus of Junius Bassus* (359).

Treasury of St. Peter's.
The Cross of Justinian II
dates from the 6th century.

Michelangelo's majestic
dome by night

THE WAY UP TO THE DOME

Access to the dome is via the right side of the portico. The first part of the ascent, from ground level to the terrace above the central nave (at the base of the dome), can be made on foot or by elevator.

The view from the balustrade is fantastic: Bernini's colonnade in the foreground, the scintillating Tiber a bit further out, and the rest of the city in the distance all create a very harmonious scene.

Passing to the interior, the gallery which runs along the drum of the dome, 53 meters above the basilica floor offers impressive views: Bernini's baldacchino, which is as tall as a building, looks to be a small scale model.

The last part of the climb goes between the two superimposed round vaults which make up the dome, which curve little by little as they rise to the top. A circular balcony from the lantern looks out onto the unforgettable panorama of the Eternal City.

The Vatican Museums

The Vatican Palaces are really a cluster of buildings whose construction began in the Middle Ages and continued under the auspices of numerous popes. The entrance is surmounted by two large *statues of Michelangelo and Raphael* which support the coat of arms of Pius XI, during whose pontificate it was built. The doors open into a broad atrium, which leads to the *spiral ramp*, built in 1932 by Giuseppe Momo. At the top of the ramp is a *circular balcony* where the ticket office is located.

CHIARAMONTI MUSEUM

Access to this museum, either directly or through the Egyptian Museum, is from the beautiful **court-yard of the Pinecone** one of the three sections of the enormous courtyard of the Belvedere designed by Bramante. The Chiaramonti Museum is called after Pius VII (1800-1823) of the Chiaramonti family; eager to continue the work of his predecessors Clement XIV and Pius VI, he arranged for a large part of the Vatican collections to be housed here. He therefore had Antonio Canova design a

The spiral ramp which gives access to the Vatican Museums, designed by Giuseppe Momo in 1932.

Above, the Todi Mars *(V century B.C.).*

long corridor flanking the cortile della Pigna, to contain about 800 sculptures. In addition to this great corridor, called the Chiaramonti Gallery, and the adjacent Lapidary Gallery, reserved for the use of scholars, the New Wing which transversely links these galleries with the parallel Vatican Library is also part of this museum.

The Braccio nuovo is a gallery 70 meters long, bordered by numerous niches and widening into an apse in the center where an allegorical representation of the Nile has been placed, a copy of an Alexandrian original from the 1st to the 2nd centuries BC, discovered in 1513 near the Campo Marzio in the heart of Rome.

Among the other valuable statues in this section, we mention the most interesting of the Chiaramonti Museum, the Augustus of Prima Porta, named after the Roman neighborhood where it was found. The emperor is shown here in an attitude of regal domination, wearing armor finely decorated in relief. The whole figure exudes a sense of masterful resolution.

The "Braccio Nuovo" built by Raphael Stern (1817-1822).

On the right, Apoxyomenos *dates from the 1st century AD.*

PIO-CLEMENTINE MUSEUM

The Pio-Clementine Museum owes its name to Clement XIV (1769-1775) and his successor, Pius VI (1775-1799) who was responsible for its final arrangement. It consists of twelve rooms, containing mainly Roman sculptures including numerous copies of Greek originals. Access to the museum today is through the former entrance made by Clement XIV, on the opposite side to the entrance Pius VI had built later. After passing the entrance arch with the inscription "Museum Clementinum", immediately on the left the visitor can admire the famous *sarcophagus of Lucius Cornelius Scipio the Bearded* (consul in 298 BC). Crossing a circular vestibule adorned with a precious funerary altar, the visitor reaches the **Cabinet of the Apoxyomenos** on the right, called after the famous Apoxyomenos, the athlete shown using a special instrument to scrape away the oil

Hermès, *a marble copy from the time of Hadrian.*

and sand with which he had covered himself. The statue is the only copy in existence of the Greek original by Lysippus (artist of the 4th century BC). The visitor then immediately finds himself in the **Octagonal Belvedere Courtyard**, not to be confused with the large Belvedere Courtyard that lies between the Library and the Lapidary Gallery.

Beneath the portico surrounding the courtyard, Canova closed off four small areas known as gabinetti (cabinets) which house some of the Vatican Museums, best known statues. These are: the **Cabinet of the Belvedere Apollo**, with a marble copy of the bronze 4th-century BC *Apollo* that came to light at the end of the 15th century and was set here by Julius II together with several other statues which formed the first nucleus of the Vatican Museums collection. The **Cabinet of the Laocoon** contains the celebrated group of *Laocoon* and his sons being strangled by sea serpents which could have been inspired by one of the most famous tales from Virgil's Aeneid. This is an original work by three sculptors from the island of Rhodes,

The Gallery of Maps.

The courtyard of the Pinecone. In the foreground, the Sphere within a Sphere (1990) by Arnaldo Pomodoro.

The Belvedere Apollo.

The Laocoon
(Ist century B.C.).

Hagesander, Athenodorus and Polydorus, and dates to 100 BC. It was found in 1506 on the Esquiline Hill. The **Cabinet of the Hermes** displays the statue of *Hermes*, a copy of an original attributed by many to Praxiteles (4th century BC). It also contains a precious Greek original dating back to the 5th century BC, representing the *head of Minerva*. The **Cabinet of Perseus** contains three statues sculpted by Antonio Canova to replace three ancient statues depicting the same subjects that were taken to Paris in 1800 after the signing of the Treaty of Tolentino between Pius VI and Napoleon Bonaparte. They show *Perseus* and two wrestlers, *Kreugas and Damoxenos*, sculpted according to the neo-classical ideals and faithfully inspired by the great examples of Greco-Roman art.

Next is the **Room of the Animals**, filled with statues of various kinds of animals many of which were drastically restored in the 18th century.

Proceeding to the right, the visitor reaches the long **Gallery of the Statues**. Many of them are

truly remarkable. We limit ourselves to pointing out the copies of two originals by Praxiteles, the greatest Greek sculptor of the 4th century BC, the *Apollo* called *Sauroktonos* because he is shown in the act of killing a lizard and a Silenus, respectively in the rows on the right and on the left on entering.

This room leads into the **Gallery of the Busts**, containing an interesting series of busts many of which are Roman originals. Indeed, the Romans excelled at this type of sculpture. The group known as *Cato and Portia*, which dates to the first century BC and shows a Roman married couple, is famous. Returning to the Gallery of the Statues, the visitor turns right down a passage adorned with a *bas-relief* from the funerary stele of a young athlete, a precious Greek original which dates to the 5th century BC. He then enters the **Cabinet of the Masks**, a small square room elegantly decorated with mosaic paving from Hadrian's sumptuous villa near Tivoli. Indeed, the mosaics represent *theatrical masks* and a delightful *countryside scene with animals*.

The Round Room designed by Simonetti.

The Gallery of the Candelabra.

The Belvedere Torso *(Iˢᵗ century BC).*

Leaving the Gallery of the Statues and once again crossing the Room of the Animals, the visitor reaches the **Room of the Muses** which owes its name to the statues of seven of these nine famous mythological figures, patronesses of the arts, exhibited here with the statue of their leader, the god Apollo of the Muses. The group set against the wall consists of Roman copies of 3ʳᵈ century BC Greek originals from Tivoli. In the center is the well-known Belvedere Torso, a highly celebrated Hellenistic fragment dating to the 1ˢᵗ century BC, signed by the Athenian Apollonius and discovered at the end of the 15ᵗʰ century in Campo de' Fiori, in Rome. It is seated on a lion skin; headless and limbless, (only the thighs remain), it nonetheless demonstrates an exceptional knowledge of anatomy and a vibrant feeling of life. The greatest Renaissance artists, starting with Michelangelo and Raphael, expressed

Perseus, *a neoclassical work by Canova.*

deep admiration for this fragment which is thought to portray Hercules.

The **Round Room** follows. In the center is a vast monolithic *porphyry basin*, more than 4 meters in diameter. The **Greek Cross Room** follows. Here two majestic porphyry sarcophagi belonging to two eminent women of Constantine's family are on view: the *sarcophagus of St. Helen*, the Emperor's mother, decorated with scenes of battles between Roman horsemen and barbarians and busts of Constantine and the saint, and the *sarcophagus of Constantia*, the Emperor's daughter, adorned with cupids harvesting grapes among vine tendrils.

The porphyry sarcophagus of St. Helen, the Emperor Constantine's mother.

THE VATICAN APOSTOLIC LIBRARY

It was founded by Sixtus IV in 1475 and set up in the long wing created by Pirro Ligorio in 1587 at the behest of Sixtus V. It is divided into several sections; the first, for those coming from the Sistine Chapel, is **Pius IX's Hall of Addresses**, in the center of which the show-case displaying objects found in the excavations of Pompei in 1849 is of considerable interest.

Next to it is the circular **Chapel of St. Pius V**, whose form corresponds to that of two chapels

The Vatican Library, foremost in Europe for the antiquity of its manuscripts and rare biographies.

One of the globes kept in the Vatican Apostolic Library.

Borgia Apartment, Room of the Saints.
St. Catherine of Alexandria's disputation with the Emperor Maximinus, by Pinturicchio - Detail.

located on the floors above and below. It contains objects from the treasury of the *Sancta Sanctorum*, the private chapel of the popes in the Lateran where important relics set in very valuable reliquaries were kept.

The **Room of the Addresses of Leo XIII** (1878-1903) and **St. Pius X** (1903-14) follows, where many letters of congratulation to these popes are kept. Continuing from the Chapel of St. Pius V, a small room can be observed on the left of the Room of the Addresses: the extremely valuable Roman fresco of the *Aldobrandini Wedding*, one of the gems of the Vatican, is preserved here. The long gallery continues with the **Room of the Papyruses**, so called because it contains a series of papyrus scrolls of the early Middle Ages (6th-9th centuries).

The next room, the Christian Museum, founded by Benedict XIV in 1756, exhibits important Christian antiquities including glass, bronze, silver and ivory objects from the Roman catacombs. This is in fact where the Library itself begins, with the **Gallery of Urban VIII**, which contains a collection of astronomical instruments. The two sections called the **Sistine Rooms** follow: on the dividing wall between the first and second room, on the side of the latter is a fresco portraying the *Transportation of the Obelisk to St. Peter's Square* (1586). On the right of the gallery is the great *Sistine Hall*, the heart of the library. The visitor then proceeds to the sections of the corridor called the Pauline Rooms, designed during the pontificate of Paul V, that is, in the first two decades of the 17th century.

Next is the **Alexandrine Room** (called after Alexander VIII) opposite the exit of the Braccio Nuovo, which was created in 1690.

The **Clementine Gallery** follows it owes its name to Clement XII (1730-40).

THE BORGIA APARTMENT

The six rooms forming the Borgia apartment are: 1. **The room of the Sibyls**; 2. **The room of the Creed**; 3. **The room of Liberal Arts**; 4. **The room of the Saints**; 5. **The room of the Mysteries**; 6. **The room of the Pontiffs**. Only the 4th and 5th rooms were painted by Pinturicchio. In the fourth, the most beautiful of all, the artist gracefully represented the stories of some of the martyrs: the dispute of St. Catherine, the Legend of St. Barbara, the Legend of St. Susan, the Visit of St. Anthony to St. Paul the Hermit, and the Martyrdom of St. Sebastian. In the fifth, the Room of the Mysteries, in the lunettes are painted the mysteries of the Resurrection, Epiphany, Nativity, Annunciation, Ascension, Pentecost and Assumption. Worthy of note in the Resurrection is the portrait of Alexander VI. The apartment was built for Alexander VI Borgia (1492-1503). In 1527, during the Sack of Rome, it was seriously damaged by fierce soldiers of the Bourbons and it is to the credit of Leo XIII that he had it restored in 1889. In 1973 Paul VI was responsible for creating a religiously oriented **Modern Art Gallery**, using fifty-five rooms starting with the Borgia appartments. It contains more than 800 works by the most important artists from the 19th century to the present day.

Room of the Segnatura. The Disputation of the Sacrament *celebrates the triumph of the Church and the Christian faith. Raphael painted this fresco while he was still young, already displaying full and mature mastery of his artistic talent.*

Religious Modern Art Collection. Ecce Homo, *by Georges Rouault (1946).*

RAPHAEL ROOMS AND LOGGIAS

In 1508, while Michelangelo was beginning the decorations of the ceiling in the Sistine Chapel, Pope Julius II commissioned Raphael, who was still very young but already the idol of Patrician Rome, to cover the walls of the four vast rooms of his new residence with large frescoes.

The visit begins with the **Hall of Constantine**, reached through an external passage looking over the Belvedere Courtyard. This room is dedicated to the emperor who, in 313, decreed freedom of worship for the Christians. It was painted after the artist's death. The decoration should be attributed to his pupils Giulio Romano and Francesco Penni.

The Cappella Niccolina is called after Pope Nicholas V Parentuccelli. It is located in the tower of Innocent III, one of the oldest monuments in the Vatican Palaces.
The frieze, painted in 1451, is the work of Beato Angelico and illustrates the histories of St. Stephen and St. Lawrence.

From here, a door in the wall to the left of the Battle of Constantine leads to **Raphael's Loggias** which face the San Damaso Courtyard. They are not open to the public; we will therefore recall only their most essential features. The general concept of the decoration is attributed to Raphael, who planned a *series of biblical scenes* portrayed in panels above the small vaults of the arcades (the famous *Bible* of Raphael). The decorative cornice inspired by the Domus Aurea (Emperor Nero's Golden House) is covered with stucco and ornamental motifs in fresco and so-called "*grotesques*".

Access to the **Chapel of Nicholas V** is from the Hall of Constantine. It was adorned with frescoes by Beato Angelico (1448-1450) in which the master clearly narrates the stories of the two proto-martyrs Stephen and Lawrence, creating richly human scenes with great formal

balance. The **Room of Heliodorus** follows. It was decorated between 1512 and 1514, by which time Raphael had completely mastered his technique. The room takes its name from the fresco on the wall of the entrance which depicts the *Expulsion of Heliodorus from the Temple in Jerusalem* for sacrilegiously attempting to steal the temple treasure.

Proceeding to the left, the visitor can admire the famous scene of the *Miracle of Bolsena*, masterfully arranged above a window. The episode illustrated took place in Bolsena in 1263: while a priest was celebrating Mass, tormented by doubts about the real presence of Christ in the consecrated host, he suddenly saw drops of blood dripping from it which stained the corporal. The fourth and last scene in the Room of Heliodorus is the *Deliverance of St. Peter from Prison*. Once again the artist has found a brilliant solution to the problem created by the presence of a window: in the lunette above, the apostle's cell penetrated by an angel shining with light is portrayed. In contrast, on either side the jailers lie on two flights of steps, stunned by the impact of the heavenly messenger's sudden appearance.

The visitor then moves on into the **Room of the Segnatura**, so called because it was the meeting place of the ecclesiastical court of that name. This room was the first in which Raphael painted his frescoes, between 1509 and 1511, and it is particularly important because they are almost entirely the master's own work. The *Disputation of the Blessed Sacrament*

A Swiss guard on duty in the Raphael Loggias. Raphael made this Loggia and the peristyle with architraves between 1517 and 1519. Today it gives access to the Secretariat of State.

The School of Athens *is one of the most important celebrations of classical culture.*

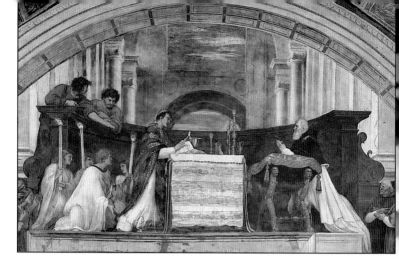

The Raphael Rooms.
The Miracle at Bolsena.

on the great wall opposite the entrance is a broad and serene composition, suffused with warm light. The fresco above the window, to the left as one observes the Disputation, illustrates three of the cardinal virtues, *Fortitude, Prudence, and Temperance*; beneath, two monochromatic scenes (that is, of a single color) next to the window, represent the fourth cardinal virtue, Justice: on the left is the Emperor Justinian delivering the Pandects (civil laws) in the 6th century; on the right, Pope Gregory IX approving the Decretals that is, the codices of ecclesiastical law (8th century).

On the entrance wall, opposite the Disputation, is another vast masterpiece in which Raphael's art is visibly even more fluent and mature than in the preceding fresco: the *School of Athens*, a celebration of human thought and knowledge. A vast, powerful basilica-like construction, inspired, it seems, by Bramante's project for St. Peter in the Vatican, is juxtaposed with an assembly of the greatest scholars and most learned philosophers of antiquity.

On the fourth and last wall on the right *Parnassus* is portrayed, the mythological mountain dedicated to Apollo and the nine Muses. The next room is the **Room of the Fire in the Borgo**, the last to which Raphael contributed, painted between 1514 and 1517. The frescoes in this room show episodes whose protagonists are Pope Leo II and Pope Leo IV who lived in the 9th century; both are portrayed with the features of Leo X, during whose pontificate they were painted. The most striking scene which has given the room its name is that of the *Fire in the Borgo*.

We will mention only some of the main frescoes in the room: on the right wall is the *Coronation of Charlemagne* by Leo III, a fresco attributed to Penni. On the left, is the *Naval Victory of Leo IV over the Saracens at Ostia* (849); on the window wall, *the Oath of Leo III*. It is attributed to Giulio Romano and by some, to Perin del Vaga.

The Raphael Rooms.
The Liberation of
St. Peter from prison.

The Sistine Chapel

The Sistine Chapel.
The Prophet Isaiah
(detail of the vault).

Between 1475 and 1483, Sixtus IV commissioned Giovanni de' Dolci to build the **Sistine Chapel**. He wanted this essential building to be architecturally isolated, virtually inaccessible from the exterior, as it were fortified. Its decoration was begun in 1482 and it transformed the severe, almost bare chapel into a precious picture gallery of 15th- and 16th-century Italian Renaissance painting. It was Pope Sixtus IV himself who commissioned some of the best painters of the time such as Perugino, Botticelli, Ghirlandaio and Cosimo Rosselli to illustrate the parallel narratives of the Old and New Testaments which face one another on the central strip of both walls. The **Life of Moses** (Old Testament) on one side and the **Life of Christ** (New Testament) opposite, were therefore painted parallel to one another on the two lateral walls. Thus **The Journey of Moses**, attributed to Pinturicchio, corresponds on the opposite side to the **Baptism of Jesus** which was certainly painted by Pinturicchio; in addition to the classical Christian symbolism, Roman monuments can be recognized on the hills in the background. The next pictures are the work of Botticelli: the biblical series on the left includes **Moses with Jethro's daughters**, and in the Gospel sequence on the right, **The Temptation of Christ** and **The Healing of the Leper**.

Continuing, the **Crossing of the Red Sea** by Cosimo Rosselli, on the side dedicated to he Old Testament. Opposite is The **Calling of the first Apostles**, by Ghirlandaio, Michelangelo's master.

Next in the sequence on one side is **Moses receiving the Tablets of the Law**, which he broke after realizing that the people of Israel were dancing round the golden calf in adoration, and on the other, **The Sermon on the Mount**, both by Rosselli. The biblical episode of **Korah, Dathan**

The Sistine Chapel.
Original Sin
(detail of the vault).

and Abiram is another work by Botticelli, facing **The Delivery of the Keys to St. Peter**, painted by Perugino, Raphael's master. On the left at the end of the series of frescoes on the lateral walls we find **The Testament** and **Death of Moses** by Luca Signorelli, while on the right is one of Cosimo Roselli's greatest works, **The Last Supper**.

In 1508, Julius II, ever eager for new enterprises, ordered the young Michelangelo to paint the **ceiling** of the Sistine Chapel. The gigantic work began in May 1508 and was completed on All Souls Day 1512. The immense challenge posed by the vast size of the surface of the vault to be covered (an area of at least 800 square meters) and its bareness was brilliantly overcome by Michelangelo with an ingenuity that reveals the rich complexity of his artistic genius. In fact, he covered the actual architecture by painting over it an architectural structure in which he set the various figurative elements with an amazing three-dimensional effect. The artist incomparably combined painting, sculpture and architecture, making the most of the curves of the vault to fit his powerful figures into the scenes.

In the center of the complex design are a sequence of nine panels showing *Episodes from Genesis*, from the main altar to the entrance wall. They are flanked by the famous *ignudi* (nudes) and portray respectively: the **Separation of Light and Darkness**, the **Creation of the Sun, the Moon and Plants**; the **Separation of the Earth and the Water**; the **Creation of Adam**. This is the central scene of the cycle, also from the pictorial point of view. The artist expresses the sublime act of creation by the simple touch of finger tips through which a real charge of vitality seems to flow from the Creator to Adam. The **Creation of Eve** and the **Original Sin** follow, original sin is a scene divided into two parts by the tree around which is coiled the serpent with the bust of a woman; twisting to the left, she invites Adam and Eve to pick the forbidden fruit. On the right, cause and effect are visibly related in the drama of the expulsion from the Garden of Eden.

Fresco of the vault of the Sistine Chapel.
The Creation of Adam.

The Ceiling of the Sistine Chapel

1) *Separation of Light and Darkness.*
2) *Creation of the Sun, the Moon and plants*
3) *Separation of the earth and the water*
4) *Creation of Adam.*
5) *Creation of Eva.*
6) *Original Sin.*
7) *Noah's Sacrifice.*
8) *Noah's Flood.*
9) *Drunkenness of Noah.*
10) *Gioele*
11) *Eritrean Sybil.*
12) *Ezechele.*
13) *Persian Sybil.*
14) *Geremia.*
15) *Libyan Sybil.*
16) *Daniele.*
17) *Cuman Sybil.*
18) *Isaia.*
19) *Delphic Sybil.*

Fresco of the vault of the Sistine Chapel.
The creation of trees and plants (detail).

Below. A religious ceremony in the Sistine Chapel with the Pope and Cardinals.

Outside the scene of earthly paradise, is **Noah's Sacrifice**. This episodes celebrates his gratitude after surviving the catastrophe and is chronologically later than the following scene of the Flood, a harmonious panel thronged with figures and episodes. Lastly, the **Drunkenness of Noah** ends the powerful sequence on the vault on a note of bitter pessimism about the wretchedness of human nature.

The **Prophets and Sybils** between the triangular spaces at the curve of the vault are the largest figures in this monumental work; they are seated on solemn high-backed chairs and accompanied by angels and cherubs. **Jesus' Forefathers** are shown in the lunettes above the windows and in the triangular "spandrels", while the four corner spandrels are painted with particularly dramatic **Episodes from the Old Testament**, concerning the salvation of the people of Israel.

A good 23 years passed, during which the Christian world was torn apart by the Lutheran

Conclaves in the Sistine Chapel

The Sistine Chapel, normally crowded with tourists, is closed to the public when it is the site of a **conclave**, convened after the death of a pope in order to elect a new pope. The Sistine Chapel became the site of conclaves soon after it was completed in the late 15th century. Its compact and well-fortified structure made it especially well suited to the secrecy of this elective assembly. In later centuries it shared this role as the site of conclaves with the Quirinale, which had been a papal

residence since the 16th century. However, after Rome was taken by Italian troops in 1870 and the popes voluntarily isolated themselves inside the Vatican, the Sistine Chapel regained its privileged position as the exclusive site for the election of the pontiff.

A unique tradition of the conclave requires that the results of the votes be communicated to the outside world by means of the smoke from the burning of the ballots after each vote. If the result is negative, the smoke rising out of the Chapel's chimney is black, thanks to the addition of a special substance; when there is at last a positive result, only the ballots are burned, which produce the eagerly awaited white smoke.

Reformation and Rome suffered the terrible Sack of 1527, before Michelangelo painted the **Last Judgement** on the wall behind the main altar. This unique masterpiece is overwhelming and dominated by the splendid audacity of its author who put his whole self into it. The Last Judgement, a compendium of the Divine Comedy and the pictorial explosion of the "Dies irae", commissioned by Pope Paul II, was begun by Michelangelo in 1535 and completed in 1541. Three hundred figures swarm in a composition which has an amazing coherence and clarity and in which space is organized into a real architectural structure of figures. Christ, the implacable judge, dominates this grandiose scene, his right arm raised in the act of condemnation. His words, "Depart from me, you cursed!" are not spoken, are not written, but they are tangibly felt. The Virgin beside him is the ever-living link between Christ and humanity. The other figures in the judge-

The Last Judgement, *by Michelangelo.*

The Last Judgement. *Detail. A damned soul.*

Between 1980 and 1994, major restoration work was done on the ceiling frescoes and the Last Judgement, which attracted much attention all around the world.
In fact, the intense cleaning effort that removed the heavy layer of dust and lampblack that had been deposited on the painting over the years, as well as the animal glues used during clumsy restoration attempts in the 18th century, brought to light unexpectedly vivid colors that led some scholars to reconsider their theory that drawing prevailed over color in Michelangelo's painting. Such a drastic return to the original conditions gave rise to a debate between those who believe that any restoration effort must take into account the fourth dimensioni of time by retaining the patina of age and those who consider it more important to reconstruct the work of art philologically, insofar as this is possible, in all its original reality.

Above. Christ the Judge, *detail.*

The Sistine Chapel. The creation of the Sun and the Moon *(detail of the vault).*

ment are the prophets, apostles and the martyrs. On the Messiah's right are the elect; on his left, the damned. Between the two lunettes, hosts of angels in heaven bring the symbols of the Passion. Below, on the left, is the scene of the resurrection of the dead: a group of angels in the center, bearing the Book of Judgement, blow trumpets, while the dead stir from gaping tombs to find themselves in the Valley of Jehoshaphat. As the good rise to heaven amidst the impotent rage of demons, the wicked are precipitated into the abysses where Charon shoves them out of his boat and Minos, the judge of hell awaits them.

THE VATICAN PICTURE GALLERY

The pictures exposed in the Vatican Picture Gallery are of exceptional interest: they are part of a collection begun by Pope Pius VI (1775-1799) which underwent various removals before being worthily housed in this functional building. Today the Picture Gallery contains about five hundred works between pictures and tapestries, arranged in the fifteen rooms which compose it according to chronological order: from the Byzantines and early Italians of 1100-1300, whose works are exposed in the 1st room, we arrive, in fact, to the artists of 1700 and the beginning of 1800. However, the nucleus of the collection is made up by the works of the greatest masters of the Italian Renaissance, of a really inestimable value. We shall limit ourselves to noting only the principal works exposed:

1st Room - **Early Italians and Byzantines** - A notable work is the *Last Judgment* of the Roman Benedictine school of the second half of the 11th century, on a tableau of a circular shape, the work of Giovanni and Niccolò.

2nd Room - **Giotto and followers** - At the centre dominates the *Polyptych* (that is, a large altar painting composed in several parts) called "Stefaneschi", from the name of the Cardinal who coimmissioned it from Giotto, who executed it with the assistance of some of his pupils. The work, recently recomposed, at the

The section of the Vatican Museums which houses the Vatican Picture Gallery built by Luca Beltrami in 1932.

The Angel Musicians by Melozzo da Forlì.

Giotto. Polittico Stefaneschi. *Tempera on wood. (1315).*

Raphael. The Madonna of Foligno *(1512).*

sides represents scenes from the lives of Sts. Peter and Paul, while at the center is the solemn figure of the benedicting Redeemer, seated on the throne between two wings of angels and adored by the same Cardinal Stefaneschi, represented below to the left.

3rd Room - **Beato Angelico** - Here are exposed some very small tableaux by this famous 15th century painter, among which are two episodes of the life of *St. Nicholas of Bari*, of an almost miniature nature, and the celebrated, most delicate *Virgin and Child, among Sts. Domenic, Catherine and Angels*, also is of tiny dimensions. The room furthermore presents three large polyptychos, among which the two interesting ones on the side walls: on the left the *Coronation of the Virgin* by Filippo Lippi, on the right the *Virgin handing the girdle to St. Thomas* by Benozzo Gozzoli, both influenced by Angelico's art.

4th Room - **Melozzo da Forlì** - The room is dominated by the large fresco which the artist had executed in the Vatican Library, later removed and placed on canvas, in order to be better kept in the Picture Gallery rooms. It represents *Sixtus IV receiving the humanist Platina*, remarkable for the psychological acuteness of the portraits of the numerous retinue, and the harmonious sense of composition. Also unforgettable are the figures of the *musician Angels and the Apostles*, coming from the frescoed decoration of the ancient apse of the church of the Holy Apostles.

5th Room - Minor painters of the 15th century - Besides Italian artists, the room also has Flemish, French and German painters.

6th Room - 15th century polyptychs - There is a remarkable *Polyptych* by the Venetian Antonio Vivarini. There are also some individual pictures exposed in the room, among which the lovely Virgin and Child by the Venetian Carlo Crivelli, signed and dated.

7th Room - 15th century Umbrian School - The room constitutes an interesting vestibule to the following room, entirely dedicated to Raphael: it presents, in fact, works of Umbrian artists, belonging to the same region as the great painter, some of whom are particularly tied to him. Here in fact is a painting by Perugino, Raphael's master: the *Virgin and Child and four Saints*, and a picture by Giovanni Santi, Raphael's father, representing *St. Jerome*.

Raphael,
The Transfiguration.

8th Room - Raphael - The room houses three of the most famous paintings and ten tapestries of the great master from Urbino.

On the large wall in front of the entrance we can admire the three great paintings. On the right is the *Coronation of the Virgin*, an early work of the artist, painted in 1503. On the left is the *Foligno Madonna*, which Raphael executed in Rome in 1512, at the time of the greatest splendour of his art.

At the centre, finally, is exposed the celebrated **Transfiguration**, which Raphael left unfinished at his sudden death which struck him down in 1520, at the age of only thirty-seven. The painting was exposed in the Sistine Chapel, before the deeply moved Romans, during the artist's funeral. It was later completed in the lower part, rather dark and agitated, in obvious contrast to the stupendous immateriality of the upper part, by Giulio Romano and Francesco Penni, two of Raphael's principal pupils.

9th Room - Leonardo da Vinci - The visitor is impressed by *St. Jerome* by Leonardo da Vinci, left unfortunately unfinished, like many, too many works

St. Jerome by Leonardo da Vinci: an incomplete work by the great master which dates to the early 1480's.

Guido Reni,
St. Matthew the
Evangelist *(1622)*.

Another modern building, created in 1970 by architects Tullio and Vincenzo Passarelli at the behest of Pope John XXIII, houses the interesting collections from the Musei Lateranensi. They are divided into three sections: the Museo Gregoriano Profano, with works and materials from archeological excavations done in the former Pontifical State, divided into two sections (Section I: Roman copies and reworkings of Greek originals; Section II: Roman sculpture, 1ˢᵗ century BC - 2ⁿᵈ century AD); the Museo Pio Cristiano, founded by Pius IX in 1854, which for the most contains materials from the catacombs and ancient Christian churches, and the Museo Missionario Etnologico, containing countless objects of a sacred nature from all around the world.

of that genial artist, writer and scientist of the Renaissance.

In front of this is a precious painting by another great artist who lived between the 15th and 16th centuries: the *Burial of Christ* by the Venetian Giovanni Bellini or "Giambellino".

10th Room - **Titian, Veronese and various 16th century artists** - The room is dominated by the immense *Madonna de' Frari*, a typical work of the most representative painter of Venice, Titian.

11th Room - **Muziano and Barocci** - The most important works representing Roman "Mannerism" are on display here; this is the school that followed the "manner" of greats Raffaello and Michelangelo. The most famous artists include Ludovico Carracci, Giorgio Vasari, Cavalier d'Arpino, Girolamo Muziano and Federico Barocci stand out, both notable representatives of the Roman artistic circle.

12th Room - **Baroque painters** - This Room, of an octagonal shape, presents paintings of considerable dimensions of the most representative figures of the 17th century. The visitor is struck above all by the *Deposition of Christ from the Cross* by Caravaggio although known through countless reproductions, the painting, seen directly, reveals a really magical luminosity which no reproduction, however perfect, could express. There are other very estimable works exposed in the same room: the *Crucifixion of St. Peter*, work of Guido Reni. Another very famous painting exposed in this Room is the *Communion of St. Jerome* by Domenichino.

13th Room - **Painters of the 17th and 18th centuries** -We note *Saint Francis Xavier* painted by the Flemish artist Anton Van Dyck. Here we found the great *Virgin and Child* by Carlo Maratta and two paintings of Peter of Cortona.

14th Room - **Painters of various nationalities of the 17th and 18th centuries**. Very popular is the *Virgin and Child* by Sassoferrato and the *Portrait of Clement IX*, the masterpiece of Carlo Maratta.

15th Room - **Portraits from the l6th to the 19th centuries** - We shall mention the elegant *Portrait of George V of England* by Sir Thomas Lawrence.

16th, 17th, 18th Rooms - **Painters of the 19th and 20th centuries**.

INSIDE VATICAN CITY

To have at least a rough idea of the microcosm enclosed within the precinct of the Vatican walls, it is worth dedicating a few hours to visiting the interior of the Leonine city (access is only permitted for guided visits organized by the information office in St. Peter's Square, in the left wing of the parvis). The Vatican City State occupies an area of 44 hectares (108.7 acres) and has a population of just over 1000 inhabitants and several thousand workmen, employees and officials who work but do not live in Vatican City. They have the task of making the small but complete mechanism of the city function. It is equipped with a radio station, a railway station, four post offices, the editorial offices of the newspaper, the printing press, and workshops of an artistic kind including the famous School of Mosaics which is responsible for maintenance of the mosaics of the basilica's altar-pieces and the tapestry workshop.

Entering the **Arco delle Campane**, the visitor finds himself in the *largo dei Protomartiri Romani*, on the spot occupied in ancient times by part of the "spina" of Nero's Circus. A marble disk marks the point where the obelisk which today stands in the center of St. Peter's Square originally stood. Next to this area is the *largo della Sagrestia*, where the entrance to the Vatican Necropolis is located.

On the left of the *Arco delle Campane*, a vast area is occupied by the **Paul VI Auditorium**, for papal audiences, designed by Pierluigi Nervi and inaugurated in 1971. It is the Vatican's most recent architectural work. In addition to its extraordinary size - it has a capacity of 12,000 - its unusual architectural style dominated by a dynamic convex

The Palace of the Governorship, designed in 1928, houses the administrative offices of Vatican City.

The Casina di Pio IV immersed in the greenery of the Vatican gardens. It was built in 1560 by Pirro Ligorio the architect of the splendid Villa d'Este in Tivoli.

The Paul VI Auditorium. Detail of Fazzini's sculpture.

parabolic ceiling in the form of a shell is impressive. At the back of the hall, behind the papal podium, towers the grandiose *sculpture of the Resurrection* made in bronze and copper by P. Fazzini in 1976.

Our visit continues from *piazza di Santa Marta*, the largest square in the Vatican from which there is an impressive view of the basilica's massive apse. In the center of the square is a delightful little garden with a fountain overlooked by the **Domus Sanctae Martae** and the **palazzo San Carlo**, built on the spot where the house of Pierluigi da Palestrina once stood, as a stone tablet recalls. Beyond the piazza di Santa Marta on the left are the the **Vatican law courts,** the **house of the Archpriest of the Vatican,** the **School of Mosaics,** the solemn and sober railway station. Continuing to the right is the **Church of Santo Stefano of the Abyssinians** of most ancient origins. Indeed, it seems to have been founded in the 6th century; in later centuries various restorations have given it its current form.

The **Palace of the Governorship** is precisely perpendicular to the basilica. Behind this grandiose palace which houses the administrative offices that see to the functioning of the City's bureaucratic machinery, are the **Gardens** which extend as far as the boundary walls of the Vatican, creating a most pleasant oasis of greenery. Access to the gardens is permitted only to guided visits, with appropriate shuttle-buses. In the gardens are the *Ethiopian College*, the *Radio Station*, set on the top of the Vatican hill, and the reconstructed *Lourdes Grotto*.

The **Casina Pio IV** (small house of Pius IV) stands in the midst of this greenery, close to the Vatican Museums. It is the work of the late-Renaissance architect, Piro Ligorio, and the seat of the *Accademia dei Nuovi Lincei* (today the Pontifical Academy of Sciences) whose members are scientists of various nationalities.

A papal audience in the Paul VI Auditorium.

The Swiss Guards

The need to be able to rely on a small but trustworthy army spurred Pope Julius II to create the Swiss Guard Corps (Cohors pedestris Helvetiorum a sacra custodia Pontificis) in 1506. An agreement with the Helvetic Confederation guaranteed a supply of soldiers, all Catholics from the German-speaking cantons, ready to serve the Pope.

Since then, there have not been many changes in the criteria for their recruitment. Great pains are still taken in selecting them today, considering as indispensable prerequisites the moral reliability, physical integrity and aesthetic appearance of the recruits.

In their colourful uniforms with slashed sleeves and puffed knickerbockers designed in the 16th century, the Swiss Guards have been involved since that time in the history of the papal State. They were formerly reinforced by the Noble Guard, recruited from among Rome's nobility, by the Palatine Guard, and by the Papal Police Force.

In 1970 Paul VI dismissed the armed papal guards but he retained the Swiss Guards who are still on duty at solemn liturgical celebrations and during celebrities' visits to the Pope and actively guard all the gates of access to Vatican City. The Swiss Guard Corps staff is nowadays of one hundred men.

Swearing-in ceremony of the Swiss Guards in the St. Damaso Courtyard.

Parade of the Swiss Guards in St. Peter's Square.

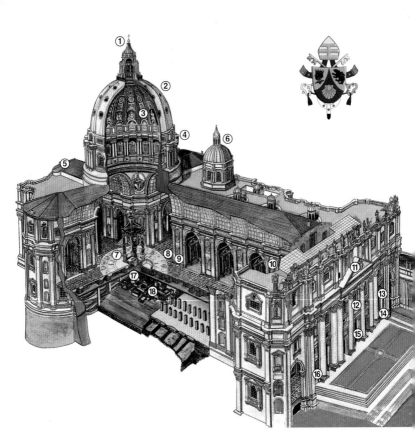

ST. PETER'S BASILICA

1. *The cross that crowns Michelangelo's dome is 136 meters tall;*
2. *The dome is 92 meters high;* 3. *The interior of the dome was decorated by Cavalier d'Arpino;* 4. *The diameter of the dome is 42 meters;* 5. *Apse with St. Peter's Throne (Bernini);* 6. *The two smaller cupolas are by Vignola;* 7. *Bernini's canopy and the high altar;* 8. *Statue of St. Longino (Bernini);* 9. *The bronze statue of St. Peter (Arnolfo di Cambio);* 10. *Michelangelo's "Pietà";* 11. *Maderno's façade is 114,69 meters wide;* 12. *The Loggia of the Benediction;* 13. *Inside the portico, the Holy Door by Vico Consorti (1949);* 14. *The way up to the dome and entrance to the Sacred Grottoes;* 15. *Inside the portico, the Central Door by Filarete (1433);* 16. *Inside the portico, the Bronze Door by Giacomo Manzù (1952-1964);* 17. *Tomb of St. Peter;* 18. *Remains of the Christian Necropoli.*

N.B.: *The asterisk* following the street coordinates (e.g., via Marghera C7*) indicates that the street is not shown on the map printed inside the front cover.*

TOURIST INFORMATION

APT, Via Parigi, 11 (B6) - ☎ 064889920. **Visitor Center,** via Parigi, 5 (B6). ☎ 0648899212. Web-site: www.romaturismo.it

ENIT - Via Marghera, 2 (C7*) - ☎ 0649711. www.enit.it
Rome Municipality, call center - ☎ 060606. www.comune.roma.it
Turistic Call Center - ☎ 0682059127. Hours: 9:30am-7:30pm.
Rome Municipality information points - PIT:

LargoGoldoni (B4*) - ☎ 0668136061. Hours: 9:15am-7:30pm;
Piazza Sonnino (D4) - ☎ 0658333457. Hours: 9:15am-7:30pm;
Via Nazionale (C5-6) - ☎ 0647824525. Hours: 9:15am-7:30pm;
Piazza San Giovanni in Laterano (E7) - ☎ 0677203535. Hours: 9:15am 7:30pm;
Castel Sant'Angelo (B3) - ☎ 0668809707. Hours: 9:15am-7:30pm;
Via dei Fori Imperiali (D5) - ☎ 0669924307. Hours: 9:15am-7:30pm;
Termini Station (C7) - ☎ 0648906300. Hours: 8:00am-9:00pm;
Piazza dei Cinquecento (C7) - ☎ 0647825194. Hours: 9:15am-7:30pm;
Santa Maria Maggiore (C6-7) - ☎ 0647880294. Hours: 9:15am-7:30pm.
The Vatican City, informations - ☎ 0669881662. www.vatican.va.
Appia Antica Card, valid for 7 days for Baths of Caracalla, Tomb of Cecilia Metella, Quintili's Villa: € 6.00.
Archeologia Card, valid for 7 days for Colosseum, Palatino, Roman National Museum, Baths of Caracalla, Tomb of Cecilia Metella, Quintili's Villa. € 20.00.
Imperial Fora Visitor Center, via dei Fori Imperiali (Largo Tempio della Pace). ☎ 066797786-702. Hours: 9:30am-6:30pm.
Museums and Monuments, ☎ 06060608. www.060608.it
Museums and archaeological sites, ☎ 0639967700. www.archeorm.arti.beniculturali.it
Roma Pass, is valid for three days: € 25.00. It can be purchased from PIT and museums. Roma Pass gives free admission to the first two museums and/or archaeological sites, full access to the public transport system, reduced tickets and discounts for the other museums, sites and events. The kit includes: *Roma Informa, Roma Map, Roma Pass Guide, Roma News.* ☎ 060608. www.romapass.it

MONUMENTS

Ara Pacis, Largo Augusto Imperatore (B4). ☎ 060608. Ticket € 7.50. Hours: 9-19. Closed on Mondays.
Baths of Caracalla, Viale Terme di Caracalla, 52. (EF6). ☎ 0639967700. Ticket € 6.00 (Appia Antica Card). Hours: from 9am to one hour before sunset.
Castel Sant'Angelo National Museum, Lungotevere Castello, 50 (C3).☎ 066819111. Ticket € 5.00. Hours: 9am-7:30pm. Closed on Mondays. www.castelsantangelo.com.
Colosseum, Piazza del Colosseo (D6). ☎ 0639967700. Ticket € 12.00 (ticket is valid also for the Palatino and Roman Forum). Hours: from 9am to one hour before sunset.
Palatino, Piazza S. Maria Nova (D5*) and Via S. Gregorio, 30 . ☎ 066990110. Ticket € 12.00 (ticket is valid also for the Colosseum and Roman Forum). Hours: from 9 am to one hour before sunset.
Pantheon, Piazza della Rotonda (C4*). ☎ 0668300230. Free entrance. Hours: 8:30am-7:30pm. On Sundays from 9am to 6pm.

Roman Forum, Largo Romolo e Remo, 5 (E5*). ☎ 0639967700. Ticket € 12.00 (ticket is valid also for the Colosseum and Palatino). Hours: from 9am to one hour before sunset.

Trajan's Markets - Museum of the Imperial Fora, Via IV Novembre, 94 (C5). ☎ 060608. Ticket € 8.50. Hours: 9am - 7pm. Closed on Mondays.

Vittoriano, Piazza Venezia (D5). ☎ 066991718. Free entrance. Hours: 9:30am-4:30pm

MUSEUMS AND GALLERIES

Ancient Art National Gallery (Palazzo Barberini), Via delle Quattro Fontane, 13, (C5-6). ☎ 064824184. Ticket € 5.00. Hours: 8:30am-7:30pm. Closed on Mondays.

Barracco Museum, Corso V. Emanuele II, 166/a (C3-4). ☎ 060608. Ticket € 5.50. Hours 9am-7pm. Closed on Mondays. www.museobarracco.it

Basilica of Santa Maria Maggiore Museum, Piazza Santa Maria Maggiore (C7). ☎ 0669886802. Ticket € 4.00. Hours: 8:30am-6:30pm.

Bioparco (Zoo). Viale del Giardino Zoologico, 20 (A5). ☎ 063608211. Ticket € 12.50. Hours: 9:30am-5pm. Sundays 9:30am - 7pm.

Borghese Gallery and Museum, Villa Borghese. Piazzale Scipione Borghese, 5 (A6*). ☎ 0632810. Visits by reservation only. Ticket € 6.50. Hours: 9am-7:00pm. Closed on Mondays. www.galleriaborghese.it

Capitolini Museums, Piazza del Campidoglio, 1 (D5). ☎ 060608. Ticket € 8.50. (ticket is valid also for the Tabularium). Hours 9am-8pm. Closed on Mondays.

Doria Pamphili Gallery, Via del Corso, 305 (C4-5). ☎ 066797323. Ticket € 10.00. Hours: 10a-5pm. Closed on Thursday.

Etruscan National Museum, Piazzale di Villa Giulia, 9 (A4*). ☎ 063226571. Entrance € 4.00. Hours: 8:30am-7:30pm. Closed on Mondays.

MACRO - Museum of Contempory Art, Via Reggio Emilia, 54 (A7). ☎ 060608. Ticket € 11.00. Hours: 11am-10pm. Closed on Mondays.

MAXXI - National Museum of the Arts of the 21th century, Via Guido Reni, 4a. ☎ 0639967350. Ticket € 11,00. Hours: tue/sun11am-7pm; thu 11-22. Closed on Mondays.

Modern Art National Gallery - GNAM, Viale delle Belle Arti, 131 (A5*). ☎ 0632298221. Ticket € 12.00. Hours: 8:30am-7:30pm. Closed on Mondays.

Museum of Palazzo Venezia, Via del Plebiscito, 118 (C4-5). ☎ 0669994318. Ticket € 4.00. Hours 8:30am-7pm. Closed on Mondays.

Museum of the Early Middle Age, Viale Lincoln, 3 (Eur). ☎ 0654228199. Ticket € 2.00. Hours: 9am-2pm. Closed on Mondays.

Palazzo delle Esposizioni, Via Nazionale, 194 (C5-6). ☎ 064745903-0639967500. Ticket € 12.50. Hours: Sun./Thu. 10-8pm; Fri./Sat. 10-10:30p,. Closed on Mondays.

Prehistoric and Ethnological Museum, Piazzale Marconi, 14 (Eur). ☎ 06549521. Ticket € 6.00. Hours: 10am-6pm. Closed on Sundays.

Roman Civilization Museum, Piazza G. Agnelli, 10 (Eur). ☎ 060608. Ticket € 7.50. Hours: 9am-2pm. Closed on Mondays.

Roman National Museum
☎ 0639967700. Ticket € 7.00. Closed on Mondays.
❖ *Baths of Diocleziano*, Viale E. De Nicola, 78 (C7). Hours: 9am-7:45pm.
❖ *Crypta Balbi*, Via delle Botteghe Oscure, 31 (D4). Hours: 9am-7.:45pm.
❖ *Palazzo Altemps*, Piazza Sant'Apollinare, 46 (C4*). Hours: 9am-7:45pm.
❖ *Palazzo Massimo*, Largo Villa Peretti, 1 (C6-7*). Hours: 9am-7:45pm.
Quintili's Villa, Via Appia Nuova, 1092. ☎ 0639967700. Ticket € 6.00.
Hours: from 9am to one hour before sunset. Closed on Mondays.
Spada Gallery, Piazza Capo di Ferro, 13 (D4*). ☎ 066874896. Ticket € 5.00.
Hours: 8:30am-7:30pm. Closed on Mondays.
Vatican Museums, Viale Vaticano, 100 (BC1). ☎ 0669884947. Ticket € 15.00.
Hours: 9am-6pm (last exit 6pm). Closed on Sundays. Visits to **Vatican
Gardens** call ☎ 0669884466. www.vatican.va

BASILICAS

Holy Cross in Jerusalem, Piazza Santa Croce in Gerusalemme, 12. ☎ 067014769
St. Agnes in Agone, Piazza Navona (C4). ☎ 0668192134
St. Clement, Piazza San Clemente (D6*). ☎ 0670451018
St. John Lateran, Piazza San Giovanni in Laterano (E7). ☎ 0669886464
St. Lawrence outside the Walls, Piazzale del Verano, 3. ☎ 06491511

St. Mary in Aracoeli, Piazza del Campidoglio, 4
(D5). ☎ 066798155
St. Mary in Cosmedin, Piazza Bocca della Verità
(E4). ☎ 066781419
St. Mary in Trastevere, Piazza Santa Maria in
Trastevere (D3). ☎ 065814802
St. Mary Major, Piazza Santa Maria Maggiore
(C7). ☎ 064881094
St. Mary of the Angels, Piazza della Repubblica
(C6). ☎ 064880812
St. Paul outside the Walls, Piazzale San Paolo. ☎ 065410341
St. Peter in the Vatican, Piazza San Pietro (C2). ☎ 0669883462
St. Peter in Vincoli, Piazza San Pietro in Vincoli, 4a (D6*). ☎ 064882865

CATACOMBS

Domitilla, Via delle Sette Chiese, 282. ☎ 065110342.
Hours: 9am-12am/2pm-5pm. Ticket € 8.00. Closed on Tuesdays.
Priscilla, Via Salaria, 430. ☎ 0686206272.
Hours: 8:30am-12pm/2:30pm-5pm. Ticket € 8.00. Closed on Mondays.
St. Agnes, Via Nomentana,349. ☎ 068610840. Hours: 9am-12pm/4pm-6pm.
Ticket € 8.00. Closed on Sundays and
Mondays.
St. Calixtus, Via Appia Antica, 110.
☎ 065136725. Hours: 9am-12am/2pm-5pm.
Ticket € 8.00. Closed on Wednesdays.
St. Sebastian, Via Appia Antica, 136.
☎ 067887035. Hours: 9am-12am/2pm-5pm.
Ticket € 8.00. Closed on Sundays.

HOTELS

Class ☆☆☆☆ L

Aldrovandi, Via U. Aldrovandi, 15 - ☎ 063223993
Aleph, Via San Basilio, 15 (B5-6) - ☎ 06422901
Ambasciatori Palace, Via Vittorio Veneto, 62 (B5-6) - ☎ 0647493
Bernini Bristol, Piazza Barberini, 23 (B6) - ☎ 064883051
Eden, Via Ludovisi, 49 (B5) - ☎ 06478121
Excelsior, Via Vittorio Veneto, 125 (B5-6) - ☎ 0647081
Exedra Boscolo Hotel, Piazza della Repubblica, 47 (C6) - ☎ 06489381
Grand Hotel de la Minerve, Piazza della Minerva, 69 (C4) - ☎ 06695201
Hassler Hotel, Piazza Trinità dei Monti, 6 (B4-5) - ☎ 06699340
Hotel De Russie, Via del Babuino, 9 (B4-5) - ☎ 06328881
Lord Byron, Via G. De Notaris, 5 - ☎ 063224541
Majestic, Via Vittorio Veneto, 50 (B5-6) - ☎ 06421441
Parco dei Principi, Via G. Frescobaldi, 5 (A6*) - ☎ 06854421
Plaza, Via del Corso, 126 (B4/C4-5) - ☎ 0669921111
Regina Hotel Baglioni, Via Vittorio Veneto, 72 (B5-6) - ☎ 06421111
Rome Cavalieri, Via Alberto Cadlolo, 101 - ☎ 0635091
St. Regis (Grand Hotel), Via Vittorio E. Orlando, 3 (BC6) - ☎ 0647091

Class ☆☆☆☆

Atlante Garden, Via Crescenzio, 78/A (B2-3) - ☎ 066872361
Atlante Star, Via G. Vitelleschi, 34 (B2-3) - ☎ 066873233
Barocco, Via della Purificazione, 4 (B5*) - ☎ 064872001
Beverly-Hills, Largo B. Marcello, 220 - ☎ 068542141
Borromini, Via Lisbona, 7 - ☎ 06852561
Cicerone, Via Cicerone, 55/C (B3) - ☎ 063576
Claridge, Viale Liegi, 62 - ☎ 06845441
Crowne Plaza Rome St. Peter's, Via Aurelia Antica, 415 (D1-2) - ☎ 0666420
De La Ville, Via Sistina, 67 (B5) - ☎ 0667331
Dei Borgognoni, Via Del Bufalo, 126 (C5*) - ☎ 0669941505
(The) Duke Hotel, Via Archimede, 69 - ☎ 06367221
Eliseo, Via di Porta Pinciana, 30 (B5) - ☎ 064870456
Empire Palace Hotel, Via Aureliana, 39 (B6*) - ☎ 06421281
Ergife Palace, Via Aurelia, 619 - ☎ 0666440
Farnese, Via Alessandro Farnese, 30 (B3*) - ☎ 063212553
Flora, Via Vittorio Veneto, 191 (B5-6) - ☎ 06489929
Forum, Via Tor de' Conti, 25 (D5) - ☎ 066792446
Giulio Cesare, Via degli Scipioni, 287 (A3/B2-3) - ☎ 063210751
Grand Hotel Tiberio, Via Lattanzio, 51 - ☎ 06399629
Holiday-Inn Parco Medici, Via Castello della Magliana, 65 - ☎ 0665581
Holiday-Inn Rome West, Via Aurelia km. 8,400 - ☎ 0666411200
Imperiale, Via Vittorio Veneto, 24 (B5-6) - ☎ 064826351
Jolly-Hotel, Corso d'Italia, 1 (B6-7) - ☎ 0684951
Jolly-Hotel Villa Carpegna, Via Pio IV, 6 - ☎ 06393731
Londra & Cargill, Piazza Sallustio, 18 (B6)- ☎ 06473871
Massimo D'Azeglio, Via Cavour, 18 (C6/D5-6) - ☎ 064870270
Mediterraneo, Via Cavour, 15 (C6/D5-6) - ☎ 064884051
Memphis, Via degli Avignonesi, 36/A (C5*) - ☎ 06485849
Mercure Delta Colosseo, Via Labicana, 144 (D6-7*) - ☎ 06770021
Midas-Jolly, Via Aurelia, 800 - ☎ 0666396

Nazionale, Piazza Montecitorio, 131 (C4) - ☎ 06695001
Nova Domus, Via G. Savonarola, 38 (A1*) - ☎ 06399511
Palatino, Via Cavour, 213 (C6/D5-6) - ☎ 064814927
Pineta Palace, Via S. Lino Papa, 35 - ☎ 063013800
Pisana Palace, Via della Pisana, 374 - ☎ 06666901
President, Via Emanuele Filiberto, 173 (D7) - ☎ 06770121
Princess, Via A. Ferrara, 33 - ☎ 06664931
Quirinale, Via Nazionale, 7 (C5-6) - ☎ 064707
Ritz, Via Chelini, 41 - ☎ 06802291
Rivoli, Via T. Taramelli, 7 - ☎ 063224042
Royal Santina, Via Marsala, 22 (C7) - ☎ 064455241
Sant'Anselmo, Piazza Sant'Anselmo, 2 (E4) - ☎ 065745174
Savoy Hotel, Via Ludovisi, 15 (B5) - ☎ 06421551
Sheraton Golf, Viale Parco dei Medici, 165 - ☎ 0665858741
Sheraton Roma, Viale del Pattinaggio 100 (Eur) - ☎ 0654531
Summit, Via della Stazione Aurelia, 99 - ☎ 0666418010
Villa Pamphili, Via della Nocetta, 105 - ☎ 066602
Visconti Palace, Via Cesi, 37 (B3*) - ☎ 063684

Class ☆☆☆

Accademia, Piazza Accademia di San Luca, 75 (C5*) - ☎ 0669922607
Adriano, Via di Pallacorda, 2 (C4*) - ☎ 0668802451
Amalfi, Via Merulana, 278 (DE7) - ☎ 064744313
Ara Pacis, Via Vittoria Colonna, 11 (B3-4) ☎ 063204446
Arcangelo, Via Boezio, 15 (B2-3) - ☎ 066874143
Astrid, Largo Antonio Sarti, 4 - ☎ 063236371
Augustea, Via Nazionale, 251 (C5-6) - 064883589
Barrett, Largo di Torre Argentina, 47 (D4) - ☎ 066868481
Buenos Aires, Via Clitunno, 9 - ☎ 068554854
Canova, Via Urbana, 10/A (C6) - ☎ 064873314
Carriage, Via delle Carrozze, 36 (B4-5) - ☎ 066990124
Celio, Via SS. Quattro, 35/C (D6/E7) - ☎ 0670495333
City Nova, Via Due Macelli, 97 (BC5) - ☎ 066797468
Clodio, Via Santa Lucia, 10 - ☎ 063721122
Columbus, Via della Conciliazione, 33 (C2-3) - ☎ 066865435
Corot, Via Marghera, 15 (C7*) - ☎ 0644700900
Della Conciliazione, Borgo Pio, 164 (B2) - ☎ 066867910
Diana, Via Principe Amedeo, 4 (CD7) - ☎ 064827541
Europa, Via Varese, 26 (BC7) - ☎ 064462096
Fiamma, Via Gaeta, 61 (B7) - ☎ 064818436
Fontana, Piazza di Trevi, 96 (C5*) - ☎ 066786113
Genio, Via Zanardelli, 28 (C4) - ☎ 066832191
Hotel Augustea, Via Nazionale, 251 (C5-6) - ☎ 064883589
Internazionale, Via Sistina, 79 (B5) - ☎ 0669941823
King, Via Sistina, 131 (B5) - ☎ 064880878
La Residenza, Via Emilia, 22 (B5*) - ☎ 064880789
Liberty, Via Nazionale, 13 (C5-6) - ☎ 06486837
Marcella, Via Flavia, 104 (B6) - ☎ 0642014591
Mercure Corso Trieste, Via Gradisca, 29 - ☎ 06852021
Mercure Piazza Bologna, Via Reggio Calabria, 54 - ☎ 06440741
Miami, Via Nazionale, 230 (C5-6) - ☎ 064817180
Milani, Via Magenta, 12 (C7) - ☎ 064457051

Nizza, Via Massimo D'Azeglio, 16 (C6) - ☎ 064881061
Oxford, Via Boncompagni, 89 (B6) - ☎ 064203601
Piccadilly, Via Magna Grecia, 122 - ☎ 0670474858
River, Via Flaminia, 39 (A4) - ☎ 063200841
Sant'Anna, Borgo Pio, 133 (B2) - ☎ 0668801602
Teatro di Pompeo, Largo del Pallaro, 8 (C4*) - ☎ 0668300170
Trevi, Vicolo del Babuccio, 21 (C5*) - ☎ 066789563
Trinità dei Monti, Via Sistina, 91 (B5) - ☎ 066797206
Villa San Lorenzo Maria, Via dei Liguri, 7 - ☎ 064469988
Villa San Pio, Via di Santa Melania, 19 (E4) - ☎ 065745231

CAMPINGS

Aurelia Club, Via Castel di Guido, 541 - ☎ 066689097
Fabulous, Via Cristoforo Colombo km 18 - ☎ 065259354

Flaminio, Via Flaminia Nuova, 821
☎ 063332604
Happy, Via Prato della Corte, 1915
☎ 0633626401
Roma, Via Aurelia, 831 km 8,100 - ☎ 066623018
Seven Hills, Via Cassia, 1216
☎ 0630310826
Tiber, Via Tiberina, km 1,400
☎ 0633610733

RESTAURANTS AND "TRATTORIE"

In restaurants marked with ★ one spends no more than 35 euro*.
In restaurants marked with ★★ one spends from 35 to 50 euro*.
In restaurants marked with ★★★ one spends from 50 to 65 euro*.
In restaurants marked with ★★★★ one spends more than 65 euro*.
Wines excluded.

★★　　　**Accademia 90,** Vicolo della Renella, 90 (D3*) - ☎ 065896321
★★★★　**Agata e Romeo**, Via C. Alberto, 45 (CD7) - ☎ 064466115
★★★★　**Alberto Ciarla**, Piazza San Cosimato, 40 (E3) - ☎ 065818668
★★★★　**Andrea**, Via Sardegna, 28 (B6) - ☎ 064821891
★★★★　**Antico Arco,** Piazzale Aurelio, 7 (D2) - ☎ 065815274
★★★　　**Antico Bottaro,** Passeggiata di Ripetta, 15 (B4*) - ☎ 063236763
★　　　　**Antico Falcone**, Via Trionfale, 60 (A1-2) - ☎ 0639743385
★★★　　**Baby**, Via U. Aldrovandi, 15 - ☎ 063223993
★★　　　**Bacaro**, Via degli Spagnoli, 27 (C4*) - ☎ 066864110
★★★★　**(Dal) Bolognese**, Piazza del Popolo, 1 (B4) - ☎ 063611426
★★★★　**Café Romano,** Via Borgognona, 41 (B4-5) - ☎ 0669981500
★★★★　**Camponeschi**, Piazza Farnese, 50 (D3) - ☎ 066874927
★★　　　**(La) Carbonara**, Piazza Campo de' Fiori, 23 (D3) - ☎ 066864783
★★　　　**(Il) Cardinale,** Via delle Carceri, 6 (C3*) - ☎ 066878430
★★★★　**Casina Valadier,** Piazzale Bucarest (A4*) - ☎ 0669922090
★★★　　**Celestina ai Parioli**, Viale Parioli, 184 - ☎ 068079505
★★★　　**(Al) Ceppo**, Via Panama, 2 - ☎ 068419696
★★★　　**(Da) Cesare,** Via Crescenzio, 13 (B2-3) - ☎ 066861227
★★　　　**Cesarina**, Via Piemonte, 109 (B6) - ☎ 064880828
★★　　　**Chalet del Lago,** Piazza Terracini - ☎ 065913743
★★★　　**Charly's Sauciere**, Via di S. Giovanni in Lat., 270 (D6/E7) - ☎ 0670494700
★★★★　**Checchino dal 1887**, Via Monte Testaccio, 30 (F4) - ☎ 065746318

★★★★ **Checco er Carrettiere**, Via Benedetta, 10 (D3*) - ☎ 065800985

★★ **(Al) Chianti**, Via Ancona, 17 (B7*) - ☎ 0644250242

★★ **(Il) Ciak,** Vicolo del Cinque, 21 (D3*) ☎ 065894774

★ **(Il) Colonnato**, Piazza del S.Uffizio, 8 (C2*) - ☎ 066865371

★★ **Colline Emiliane**,Via degli Avignonesi, 22 (C5*) - ☎ 064817538

★★★ **Consolini**, Via Marmorata, 28 (EF4) - ☎ 0657300148

★★★★ **(Il) Convivio**, Vicolo dei Soldati, 31 (C4*) - ☎ 066869432

★★★ **Coriolano**, Via Ancona, 14 (B7*) - ☎ 0644249863

★★ **(Il) Cortiletto**, Piazza Capranica, 76 (C4*) - ☎ 066793977

★★★ **Costanza**, Piazza del Paradiso, 63 (C4*) - ☎ 066861717

★★ **(Il) Drappo**, Vicolo del Malpasso, 9 (C3*) - ☎ 066877365

★★ **Duke's,** Viale Parioli, 200 - ☎ 0680662455

★★ **(L') Eau Vive**, Via Monterone, 85 (C4) - ☎ 0668801095

★★ **Edoardo**, Via Lucullo, 2 (B6) - ☎ 06486428

★ **(L') Enoteca Antica,** Via della Croce, 76b (B4) - ☎ 066790896

★★★★ **(Les) Etoiles**, Via dei Bastioni, 1 (B2) - ☎ 066873233

★★★ **Evangelista**, Via delle Zoccolette, 11 (D4*) - ☎ 066875810

★★★ **Fabrizio a Trastevere**, Via Santa Dorotea, 15 (D3*) - ☎ 065806244

★★★ **Ferrara,** Piazza Trilussa, 41 (D3) - ☎ 0658333920

★★★ **Fortunato**, Via del Pantheon, 55 (C4*) - ☎ 066792788

★★ **(La) Gallina Bianca**, Via A. Rosmini, 9 (C6-7*) - ☎ 064743777

★★★ **Giovanni**, Via Marche, 64 (B6*) - ☎ 064821834

★★★ **Girarrosto Fiorentino,** Via Sicilia, 46 (B6) - ☎ 0642880660

★★★ **Girarrosto Toscano**, Via Germanico, 56 (B2) - ☎ 0639725717

★★★★ **Grand Hotel Tiberio**, Via Lattanzio, 51 - ☎ 06399629

★★★ **'Gusto**, Piazza Augusto Imperatore, 9 (B4) - ☎ 063226273

★★★★ **Hostaria dell'Orso**, Via dei Soldati, 25c (C4*) - ☎ 0668301192

★★ **Lilli,** Via Tor di Nona, 23 (C3*) - ☎ 066861916

★ **(Da) Lucia**, Vicolo del Mattonato, 2b (D3*) - ☎ 065803601

★★★ **Mariano**, Via Piemonte, 79 (B6) - ☎ 064745256

★★ **Massimo D'Azeglio**, Via Cavour, 14 (C6/D5-6) - ☎ 064814101

★★★ **(Il) Matriciano**, Via dei Gracchi, 55 (B3) - ☎ 063212327

★★ **Melarancio,** Via del Vantaggio, 43 (B4) - ☎ 063202200

★★★ **Nino**, Via Borgognona, 11 (B4-5) - ☎ 066786752

★★ **(La) Norma**, Via Flaminia Vecchia, 733 - ☎ 063330210

★★ **Osteria della Frezza,** Via della Frezza, 16 (B4*) - ☎ 063226273

★★★ **Osteria dell'Antiquario**, Piazza S. Simeone, 27 (C3*) - ☎ 066879694

★★ **Osteria dell'Ingegno,** Piazza di Pietra, 45 (C4) - ☎ 066780662

★★★ **Ostrica**, Via Tuscolana, 2086 - ☎ 067232540

★★★★ **Papà Baccus**, Via Toscana, 36 (B6*) - ☎ 0642742808

★★★★ **Papà Giovanni**, Via dei Sediari, 6 (C4*) - ☎ 0668804807

★★★ **Passetto**, Via Zanardelli, 14 (C4) - ☎ 0668803696

★★★★ **(La) Pergola - Rome Cavalieri**, Via A. Cadlolo, 101 - ☎ 0635092152

★ **Perilli a Testaccio**, Via Marmorata, 39 (EF4) - ☎ 065742415

★★★ **(Il) Peristilio,** Via Col di Lana, 10 (A3*) - ☎ 0632649022

★★★ **Piperno**, Via Monte dè Cenci, 9 (D4*) - ☎ 066861113

★★ **Pommidoro**, Piazza dei Sanniti, 44 - ☎ 064452692

★ **(Al) Pompiere**, Via S. Maria dei Calderari, 38 (D4*) - ☎ 066868377

★★ **Porto di Ripetta**, Via di Ripetta, 250 (B4) - ☎ 063612376

★★   **(Il) Posto Accanto**, Via del Boschetto, 36/A (C6*) - ☎ 064743002
★★   **Quattro Fiumi**, Piazza Navona, 37 (C4) - ☎ 066864028
★★★★ **Relais la Piscine**, Via G. Mangili, 6 - ☎ 063216126
★★★ **Robià**, Via Cicerone, 55 (B3) - ☎ 063576
★★   **Romolo**, Via di Porta Settimiana, 8 (D3*) - ☎ 065818284
★★★★ **(La) Rosetta**, Via della Rosetta, 8/9 (C4*) - ☎ 0668308841
★★★★ **(I) Sapori**, Via G. De Notaris, 5 - ☎ 063224541
★   **Scoglio di Frisio**, Via Merulana, 256 (DE7) - ☎ 064872765
★★   **(Da) Sergio,** Vicolo delle Grotte, 27 (D4*) - ☎ 066864293
★★   **Taverna Angelica**, Piazza Capponi, 6 (B2*) - ☎ 066874514
★★★ **Taverna Flavia**, Via Flavia, 9 (B6) - ☎ 064870483
★   **Taverna Giulia**, Vicolo dell'Oro, 23 (C3*) - ☎ 066869768
★★   **Terra di Siena**, Piazza Pasquino, 77 (C3*) - ☎ 0668307704
★★★★ **(La) Terrazza dell'Eden**, Via Ludovisi, 49 (B5) - ☎ 0647812752
★   **Tiepolo,** Via Tiepolo, 3/6 - ☎ 063227449
★★   **(Dal) Toscano**, Via Germanico, 58 (B2) - ☎ 0639725717
★★★★ **(El) Toulà**, Via della Lupa, 29b (C4*) - ☎ 066873750
★   **Trattoria Monti**, Via S. Vito, 13/A (D7) - ☎ 064466573
★★   **(Il) 34**, Via Mario dè Fiori, 34 (B5*) - ☎ 066795091
★   **(Al) Vantaggio,** Via del Vantaggio, 35 (B4) - ☎ 063236848
★★★ **Vecchia Roma**, Piazza Campitelli, 18 (D4) - ☎ 066864604

PUBS

Abbey, Via del Governo Vecchio, 51 (C3)
☎ 066861341
(The) Albert, Via del Traforo, 132 (C5*)
☎ 064818795
Birreria Marconi, Via Santa Prassede, 9/C
(C6*) - ☎ 06486636
Buonconsiglio, Via del Colosseo, 1/C (D6)
☎ 066791729
Caffé Novecento, Via del Governo Vecchio,
12 (C3) - ☎ 066865242
Crazy Bull, Via Mantova, 5/B (A7*)
☎ 068845975

Druid's Den, Via San Martino ai Monti, 28 (D6-7) - ☎ 0648904781
Enoteca il Piccolo, Via del Governo Vecchio, 51 (C3) - ☎ 0668801746
Four Green Fields, Via C. Morin, 42 (A2*) - ☎ 063725091
Four XXXX Pub, Via Galvani, 29 (F4) - ☎ 065757296
Lot87, Via del Pellegrino, 87 (C3) - ☎ 0697618344
Mad Jack's, Via Arenula, 20 (D4) - ☎ 0668808223
(The) Nag's Head, Via IV Novembre, 138b (C5) - ☎ 066794620
Penny Lane, Via dei Gracchi, 35/37 (B3) - ☎ 063219645
Radio Londra Café, Via di Monte Testaccio, 65/B (F4) - ☎ 065750044
Riccioli Caffé, Via delle Coppelle, 47 (C4*) - ☎ 0668210313
Rive Gauche 2, Via dei Sabelli, 43 - ☎ 064456722
Salotto 42, Piazza di Pietra, 42 (C4) - ☎ 066785804
Societé Lutece, Piazza di Montevecchio, 17 (C3*) - ☎ 0668301472
Spaten Braun, Viale America, 73 (Eur) - ☎ 065913841
Supperclub, Via dei Nari, 14 (C4*) - ☎ 0668807207
Trinity College Music Bar, Via del Collegio Romano, 6 (C4-5*)
☎ 066786472
Vinoteca Novecento, Piazza delle Coppelle, 47 (C4*) - ☎ 066833078

TRANSPORTS

BUS, METRO AND URBAN RAILWAYS

Public City Transports (A.T.A.C) - ☎ 800431784.
www.atac.roma.it
Time Integrated Ticket (BIT) valid 75 minutes from first stamping for buses and only one trip on metro and urban trains: € 1.00. **Integrated Ticket (BIG),** valid till 12pm on the day of validation for an unlimited number of journeys on buses, metro and urban trains: € 4.00. **Integrated Tourist Ticket (BTI)**, valid for three days for unlimited number of journeys on buses, metro and urban trains: € 11.00. **Integrated Weekly Pass (CIS)** valid seven days for all and any metro, bus and urban trains: € 16.00. **Integrated Monthly Pass**, valid for all and any metro, bus and urban trains: € 30.00. The daily tickets and weekly and monthly passes can be bought in tobacconists, cafés and news-stands advertising their sale.
Extra-urban busses (CO.TRA.L) - ☎ 800150008.
  Web-site: www.cotralspa.it
Metro of Rome (MET.RO) - ☎ 800431784. Hours: 8am-8pm. www.metroroma.it

STATIONS - NATIONAL STATE RAILWAYS

F.S. Trenitalia. ☎ 892021. www.trenitalia.it

AIRPORTS OF ROME

Web-site: www.adr.it
"Leonardo Da Vinci" Intercontinental Airport of Fiumicino - ☎ 0665951 - 0665953640-0665955237.
Ciampino Airport "G. B. Pastine" - ☎ 0665951

TO/FROM FIUMICINO AIRPORT "LEONARDO DA VINCI"

Trains (F.S.):
Roma Tiburtina Station - Airport Leonardo Da Vinci - Fiumicino. Departures every 15 minutes, from 6:27am to 9:27pm. Ticket: € 8.00.

Direct line, Rome Termini Station (Platforms 224) **- L. Da Vinci Airport of Fiumicino.** The **"Leonardo Express"** train leaves Rome's Termini Station daily every thirty minutes from 5:52am until 10:52pm. From Fiumicino Airport, it leaves every thirty minutes from 6:37am to 11:37pm. Tickets € 14.00.
Buses:
Leonardo Da Vinci Airport in Fiumicino. Departures from Tiburtina Station, from 12:37pm to 3:45am. From Fiumicino Airport to go to Tiburtina Station, from 1:15am to 5:00am. To go to Termini Station from 11:30pm to 5:00am. Tickets €7.00.

TO/FROM CIAMPINO AIRPORT "G. B. PASTINE"

Ciampino Airport. Every 30 minutes from (from 6:10am to 11:00pm)/to (from 6:40am to 11:40pm) Anagnina Metro Station of line A - ticket € 1.20. Line Termini Station - Ciampino Airport - ticket € 3.90.

TAXIS

RADIOTAXIS - ☎ 892192 (nazionale) - 068822 - 066645 - 064157 - 063570 - 064994

Arriving and departing at "Leonardo Da Vinci" Intercontinental Airport of Fiumicino from the historic centre (including the entire area inside the Aurelian walls) is applied a fixed rate of € 40.00, including luggage. Approximate examples of some common routes: from Rome Fleming/Corso Francia, € 45.00; from Rome-Eur, € 30.00; from Rome-Termini, € 36.00; From the Airport to Rome.

Arriving and departing at "G. B. Pastine" International Airport of Ciampino from the historic centre (including the entire area inside the Aurelian walls) is applied a fixed rate of € 30.00, including luggage. For other destinations the price is calculated by the taxi meter.

Supplements: departure from Termini Station € 2.00 - fee for a second bag € 1.00 - nights (from 10pm to 7am) € 3.50, Sundays and holidays € 1.00.

RENT A CAR

AVIS - Via Tiburtina, Km 1229 - ☎ 064131414. Fiumicino Airport - ☎ 0665011531. Ciampino Airport - ☎ 0679340195. Termini Station - ☎ 064814373.
CRISS - Via dei Prati Fiscali, 273 - ☎ 068861920. Via Aurelia, 565 - ☎ 0666541829.
EUROPCAR Via Giolitti, 34 (Termini Station) - ☎ 064882854. Fiumicino Airport - ☎ 0665010977. Ciampino Airport - ☎ 0679340387.
FREE ROME, Electric car rental - ☎ 0642013110.
HERTZ, Termini Station - ☎ 064740389. Fiumicino Airport - ☎ 0665011553.
MAGGIORE, Fiumicino Airport - ☎ 0665010678. Termini Station - ☎ 064880049.
SIXT, Fiumicino Airport - ☎ 0665953547. Ciampino Airport - ☎ 0679340838.

SCOOTERS FOR RENT

HAPPY RENT, Via Piave, 49 (B7) - ☎ 0642020675.
SCOOT A LONG, Via Cavour, 302 (C6/D5-6) - ☎ 066780206.
SCOOTERS FOR RENT, Via della Purificazione, 84 (B5) ☎ 064885485.

SHOPPING

TIME SCHEDULE:
Winter season (from October to March): from 9:00am to 1:00pm and from 3:30pm to 7:30pm. Some shops in the center of the City are open no-stop from 10:30am to 7:30pm. Shops are close on Mondays mornings. The grocery stores are closed on Thursday afternoons and specialised stores are closed on Saturday afternoons.

Summer season (from April to September): from 9:00am to 1:00pm and from 4:00pm to 8:00pm. During the Summer season the shops are closed on Saturdays afternoons. In every month of the year shops are mostly closed on Sunday days.

Via Condotti (B4-5): clothes, shoes and jewellry from the most famous Italian and foreign designers, such as *Armani* (n. 77), *Prada* (n. 88), *Gucci* (n. 8), *Bulgari* (n. 10), *Cartier* (n. 82/83), *Ferragamo* (n. 73 and 74), *Max Mara* (n. 17), *Campanile* (n. 58), *Valentino for women* (n. 12). And in **Via Bocca di Leone (B5)**, a side street, you'll find *Rocco Barocco* (n. 65a) and *Gianni Versace* (n. 23).

Piazza di Spagna (B5): if we manage to tear our gaze away from the magnificent spectacle of the splendid square and its incomparable stairway we can recognize the shop windows of some of the best known boutiques selling clothing, leather goods and shoes, among which we find *Krizia* (n. 87), *Missoni* (n. 78), *Les Copains* (n. 33) and *Dolce e Gabbana* (n. 82).

Via Borgognona (B4-5): clothes and shoes of the greatest Italian fashion designers, such as *Fendi* (n. 39), *Gucci* (n. 7b), *Laura Biagiotti* (n. 43), *Roberto Cavalli* (n. 24), *Moschino* (n. 32a), *Valentino*, (n. 61).

Via del Corso (B4/C4-5): clothes, shoes, jeans.

Via del Babuino (B4-5): antiques and clothing, such as *Emporio Armani* (n.140), *Nannini* (n. 75), *Prada* (n. 91) and *Iceberg* (n. 87).

Via Cola di Rienzo (B2-3): clothes, shoes.

Porta Portese (E3-4): characteristic flea market full of all kinds of antique, used and new items. Open every Sunday morning in the streets around Porta Portese.

TAX-FREE SHOPPING

Tourists arriving from countries not belonging to the European Union can request the refund of I.V.A. (V.A.T. which ranges from 12% to 35% on purchase price) for amounts exceeding € 155.00 spent in the same shop. To enjoy this benefit it's necessary to apply to shops that have an agreement with the organizations offering the service (Tax Free, Italy Free Shopping, Tax Free System, Euro Tax, Tax Refund). The refund can be obtained inside the shops with the proper sign, at Leonardo Da Vinci International Airport of Fiumicino, in the Customs office, or by post.

EMERGENCY TELEPHONE NUMBERS

CARABINIERI 112
FIRE BRIGADE 115
FIRST-AID 118
ITALIAN RED CROSS (CRI) AMBULANCE 065510
MEDICAL SERVICE 06570600
MUNICIPAL POLICE 0667691
POLICE - EMERGENCY 113
PUBLIC CITY TRANSPORTS (ATAC) 800431784
ROME MUNICIPALITY 060606
TRAFFIC & HIGHWAY POLICE 0664686

LIST OF STREETS ON MAP PRINTED ON THE INSIDE FRONT COVER

Abbreviations:
lg. = largo
lt. = lungotevere

p. = piazza
p.le = piazzale
pn. = ponte

v.le = viale
d. = del, delle
crv. = circonvallazione

Adda (via), A7
Adriana (piazza), B3
Albalonga (via), F8
Albania (piazza), EF5
Alberico II (via), B2-3
Alberteschi (lt. degli), D4
Alessandria (p. e via), AB7
Alfieri (via), D7
Allegri G. (via), A6
Amba Aradam (via), E7
Amelia (via), E10
Amendola G. (via), C7
Amedeo di Savoia (pn.), C3
Amedeo Ottavo (via), DE8
Andrea Doria (via), B1, A2
Angelico (viale), A2
Anguillara (lt. degli), D4
Anicia (via), DE4
Annia (via), E6
Annibaldi (via degli), D6
Anzani (largo), F3
Aosta (via), E8
Appia Nuova (via), E8-9
Aracoeli (via), D4-5
Arcione (via), C5
Ardea (via), E8
Arenula (largo), D4
Arenula (via), D4
Ariosto (via), D7
Armi (lt. delle), A3
Arnaldo da Brescia (lt.), A4
Artigiani (lt. degli), F3
Assisi (via), F10
Augusta (lt. in), B4
Augusto Imperatore (p.), B4
Aurelia Antica (via), D1-2
Aurelio (piazzale), D2
Ausoni (via degli), C9
Aventina (via), EF5
Aventino (lt.), E4
Aventino (viale), E5
Azuni D. A. (via), A4
Babuino (via del), B4-5
Baccelli G. (viale), E5-6, F5
Baccina (via), D5-6
Balbo C. (via), C6
Banchi Nuovi (via dei), C3
Banchi Vecchi (via dei), C3
Banco di Santo Spirito (v.), C3
Barberini (via), B6
Barberini (piazza), BC5
Bari (via), B8-9
Barletta (via), AB2
Barrili A. G. (via), EF2
Basento (via), A7
Bassi U. (via), E3
Bastioni (via dei), B2
Battisti C. (via), C5
Baullari (via dei), C4
Beccaria C. (via), A4
Belli G. G. (piazza), D4
Bernardino da Feltre (largo), E3
Bernini G. L. (piazza), F5

Biancamano (via), E8
Biondo F. (piazza), F3
Bissolati (via), B6
Bocca della Verità (p.), D4-5
Bodoni G. B. (via), F3-4
Boezio (via), B2-3
Boiardo (via), DE7
Bologna (piazza), A9
Boncompagni (via), B6
Bonghi R. (via), D7
Borgognona (via), B4-5
Borsieri P. (via), A2
Bossi B. (viale), F5
Botta C. (via), D7
Botteghe Oscure (v. d.), D4
Branca G. (via), EF4
Brancaccio (largo), D7
Brasile (piazzale del), B5
Britannia (via), F8
Brofferio A. (via), A3
Buenos Aires (piazza), A7
Buonarroti (via), D7
Caio Cestio (via), F4
Camozzi G. (via), A2
Campanella T. (via), A1
Campidoglio (piazza), D5
Campitelli (piazza), D4
Campo Boario (vl. del), F4
Campo dei Fiori (p.), CD4
Campo Marzio (via), BC4
Cancelleria (p. d.), C3-4
Candia (via), B1-2
Canova A. (via), B4
Capo d'Africa (via), DE6
Cappellari (via dei), C3
Cappellini A. (via), C7
Caprera (piazza), A8
Carducci G. (via), B6
Carine (via delle), D6
Carini G. (via), E2
Carlo Alberto (via) CD7
Carlo Felice (via), E8
Carrozze (via delle), B4-5
Casilina (via), DE9-10
Cassiodoro (via), B3
Castelfidardo (via), B7
Castrense (via), E8
Castro Pretorio (viale), BC7-8
Catania (via), B9
Cattaneo C. (via), C7
Catullo (via), B3
Cavalcanti (via), F2
Cavallotti F. (via), EF2
Cavour (piazza), B3
Cavour (via), C6, D5-6
Celimontana (via), DE6
Celso (via), AB8
Cenci (lt. dei), D4
Cerchi (via dei), E5
Cernaia (via), B6-7
Cerveteri (via), EF8
Cestari (via dei), C4
Cestio (ponte), D4

Chiesa Nuova (piazza della), C3
Ciambella (arco della), C4
Cicerone (via), B3
Cimarra (via), C6
Cinquecento (piazza d.), C7
Cinque Giornate (p. d.), A3
Cinque Scole (p. d.), D4
Circo Massimo (via del), E5
Claudia (via), E6
Clementi M. (via), B4
Clodio (piazzale), A2
Cola di Rienzo (via), B2-3
Collegio Romano (p.), C4-5
Colonna (piazza), C4-5
Colonna V. (via), B3-4
Colosseo (piazza e via del), D6
Conciliazione (via d.), C2-3
Condotti (via dei), B4-5
Conservatorio (via del), D4
Consolazione (via d.), D5
Coppelle (via delle), C4
Coronari (via dei), C3
Corridori (via dei), B2
Corso (via del), B4, C4-5
Cossa P. (via), B3-4
Crescenzio (via), B2-3
Crispi F. (via), B5
Croce (via), B4
Croce Rossa (piazza d.), B7
Dalla Chiesa C. A. (via), A2
Damiata (via), A3
Dandolo (via), E3
Dante (piazza), D7
Dataria (via), C5
D'Azeglio M. (via), C6
Deci (via dei), E5
Del Grande N. (via), E3
Della Rovere (piazza), C2
De Lollis C. (via), C8-9
De Nicola E. (viale), C7
Depretis A. (via), C6
Di Lauro M. (via), A9-10
Dionigi M. (via), B3-4
Donizetti G. (via), A6
Donna Olimpia (piazza e via), F1
Druso (via), EF6
Due Macelli (via del), BC5
Emanuele Filiberto (v.), D7
Epiro (piazza), F7
Equi (via degli), CD8
Eroi (piazzale degli), B1
Esquilino (piazza), C6
Etruria (via), F8
Eudossiana (via), D6
Eustachio B. (via), A8
Fabio Massimo (via), B2
Fabrizi N. (via), E3
Fabrizio G. (piazza), B8
Faleria (via), E8
Farnese (piazza), D3
Farnesina (lt. della), D3
Farsalo (via), E7
Ferrari G. (via), A3